# WELSH NARROW GAUGE

## A VIEW FROM THE PAST

### PETER JOHNSON

Ian Allan

PUBLISHING

*Front cover (main image):* Talyllyn Railway No 2 *Dolgoch* crossing Dolgoch Viaduct during the first years of the 20th century. *Commercial postcard/ Pictorial Stationery Co/Gwyn Price Collection*

*Front cover (right, top to bottom):* The Festiniog Railway's famous Tan-y-bwlch 'station mistress', Bessie Jones, was photographed in 1937, complete with single-line train staff and picture postcards. *Rev Stewart Marsh*

A view of the days in Welshpool when steam trains crossing the main road were so commonplace they could easily be ignored by passers-by. *Commercial postcard/J. Valentine/ Peter Johnson Collection*

Snowdon Mountain Railway No 2 *Enid* seen at Llanberis when newly delivered in 1896. *Commercial postcard/J. Valentine/ Peter Johnson Collection*

*Back cover (top to bottom):*The days when narrow gauge railways were common carriers are illustrated by this view of the Vale of Rheidol Railway's Devil's Bridge terminus before World War 1. In the foreground is Bagnall 2-4-0T *Rheidol* with a passenger train and passengers, and in the goods yard behind are several wagons, including some loaded with timber. The pony and trap standing in the yard provide a reminder of other modes of transport. *Commercial postcard/ E. T. W. Dennis/Peter Johnson Collection*

A Welshpool & Llanfair Light Railway cattle train at Raven Square, Welshpool. *Millbrook House Collection*

*Title page:* The Talyllyn Railway's *Dolgoch* at Rhydyronen in 1951. For the first weekend of preservation services terminated here. *P. B. Whitehouse/Millbrook House Collection*

*Below:*
The Glyn Valley Tramway's third Beyer Peacock, *Dennis*, was built in 1888 and is seen here with a mixed train on 31 May 1932. The location is the Chirk Castle estate, on the outskirts of the town. *H. C. Casserley/Millbrook House Collection*

First published 1999

ISBN 0 7110 2654 8

© Peter Johnson 1999

Published by Ian Allan Publishing

an imprint of Ian Allan Publishing Ltd, Terminal House, Shepperton, Surrey TW17 8AS.
Printed by Ian Allan Printing Ltd, Riverdene Business Park, Hersham, Surrey KT12 4RG.

Code: 9906/B

# Contents

*Right:*
Bessie Jones's husband, Will, worked for the Festiniog Railway, as a track ganger. Here the fireman appears to have a note for him.
*Gwyn Price Collection*

# Bibliography

Anderson, R. C.; *Great Orme Tramway — The First 80 years*; LRTA, 1982

Baughan, Peter E.; *A Regional History of the Railways of Great Britain: Vol 11; North and Mid Wales*; David St John Thomas Pub, 2nd edition, 1991

Boyd, J. I. C.; *Narrow Gauge Railways in North Caernarvonshire*; Oakwood Press, 1981, 1985/6 (3 vols)

Boyd, J. I. C.; *Narrow Gauge Railways in South Caernarvonshire*, Oakwood Press, 1988/9 (2 vols)

Boyd, J. I. C.; *Narrow Gauge Railways in Mid-Wales*; Oakwood Press, 1970

Boyd, J. I. C.; *The Tal-y-llyn Railway*; Wild Swan Publications, 1988

Bradley, V. J.; *Industrial Locomotives of North Wales*; Industrial Railway Society, 1992

Briwnant-Jones, G.; *Great Western Corris*; Gomer Press, 1994

Carrington, Douglas C.; *Delving in Dinorwig*; Gwasg Carreg Gwalch, 1994

Cartwright, Ralph and Russell, R. T.; *The Welshpool & Llanfair Light Railway*; David & Charles, 3rd edition, 1989

Cartwright, Ralph; *Welshpool & Llanfair Light Railway — A Collection of Pictures*; Bridge Books, 1995

Christiansen, Rex; *Forgotten Railways North and Mid Wales*; David & Charles, 2nd edition, 1984

Corris Railway Society; *A Return to Corris*; Avon-Anglia Publications, 1988

Davies, David Llewelyn; *The Glyn Valley Tramway*; Oakwood Press, 2nd edition, 1991

Green, C. C.; *The Vale of Rheidol Light Railway*; Wild Swan Publications, 1986

Grosvenor, David; *RE — Guidebook — WHR*; Festiniog Railway Co, 1998

Hindley, P.; 'A Quarry Railway at Penmaenmawr'; *Industrial Railway Record*, No 68

Hitches, Mike; *Penmaenmawr — Rails of Granite*; Irwell Press, 1990

Johnson, Peter; *Festiniog Railway — A View From The Past*; Ian Allan, 1997

Johnson, Peter; *The Heyday of the Welsh Narrow Gauge*; Ian Allan, 1997

Johnson, Peter; *Portrait of the Festiniog*; Ian Allan, 1992

Johnson, Peter; *Portrait of the Welsh Highland Railway*; Ian Allan, 1999

Johnson, Peter & Weaver, Rodney; *Great Preserved Locomotives — Talyllyn Railway No 1 Talyllyn & No 2 Dolgoch*; Ian Allan, 1987

Jones, Norman; *Snowdon Mountain Railway Llanberis*; Foxline Publishing, 1998

Jones, Reg Chambers; *Felinheli — A Personal History of the Port of Dinorwic*; Bridge Books, 1992

Lee, Charles E.; *Narrow Gauge Railways in North Wales*; Railway Publishing Co, 1945

Milner, W. J.; *The Glyn Valley Tramway*; Oxford Publishing Co, 1984

Milner, W. J.; *Rails Through the Sand — The Story of the Fairbourne Miniature Railway*; Rail Romances, 1996

Mitchell, David J. and Eyres, Terry; *The Talyllyn Railway*; Past & Present Publishing, 1996

Mitchell, Vic and Smith, Keith; *Branch lines Around Portmadoc — The Welsh Highland and Festiniog Railways 1923-46*; Middleton Press, 1993

*Rheilffordd Eryri The Welsh Highland Railway*; Festiniog Railway Co, 1994

Morgan, John Scott; *Corris — A Narrow Gauge Portrait*; Irwell Press, 1991

Potter, David; *The Talyllyn Railway*; David St John Thomas, 1990

Price, Geoff; *A Nostalgic Look at Llandudno & Colwyn Bay Trams since 1945*; Silver Link Publishing, 1997

Rolt, L. T. C.; *Railway Adventure*; Alan Sutton, 1993

Stretton, John; *The Festiniog and Welsh Highland Railways*; Past & Present Publishing, 1996

Turner, Keith; *The Llandudno & Colwyn Bay Electric Railway*; Oakwood Press, 1993

Turner, Keith; *The Snowdon Mountain Railway*; David & Charles, 1973

Turner, Susan; *The Penrhyn & Padarn Railways*; David & Charles, 1975

Wade, E. A.; *The Plynlimon & Hafan Tramway*; Twelveheads Press, 1997

Whitehouse, P. B.; *Festiniog Railway Revival*; Ian Allan, 1963

# Foreword

It is the geology that defines North Wales from a railway perspective. It is responsible for the mountains, the valleys, the lakes and, especially, the minerals, the reason for the concentration of narrow gauge railways that contribute to its international fame. And in a fairly compact area there came to be developed a variety of narrow gauge railways quite unlike any to be found anywhere else on earth.

As implied, most of the lines were mineral carriers, slate primarily, and granite. Exceptionally, the Welshpool & Llanfair Light Railway served agriculture and the Fairbourne Railway started off as a house-builder's tramway. Passenger carriage, where it existed at all, was nearly always an afterthought. Exceptions were the Rhyl Marine Lake Railway, the Snowdon Mountain Railway, the Great Orme Tramway and the Llandudno & Colwyn Bay Electric Railway, the last two being unusual in not using steam traction.

The mineral extraction industry made considerable use of the narrow gauge railway. Notable were the slate quarries at Dinorwic and Penrhyn, both having considerable main lines to transport their output from their respective quarries, in addition to internal tramways. They both (as did others) made use of the attractive 'quarry' Hunslet 0-4-0ST, supplied in various permutations. Several quarries, including the granite quarries at Penmaenmawr, also made use of the distinctive Caernarfon-built de Winton vertical-boilered locomotives.

Most of these railways survived World War 2, although lack of investment, maintenance and the advance of the internal combustion engine for road transport combined to ensure that they were ill-prepared to face the future. Of those that did survive the war, some managed to be absorbed by the railway preservation movement. Others were closed or abandoned as the demand for their services or products declined or their users' transport requirements could be met by alternative means. Whatever happened, the postwar vista turned out to be considerably different from the prewar scene.

This book, therefore, takes a clockwise tour of lines that were operating in the early 1930s, starting with the Welshpool & Llanfair Light Railway and ending with the Glyn Valley Tramway, although the photographs used are not restricted to this period, visiting also a representative selection of internal quarry systems. This device has the distinction of placing the Welshpool & Llanfair Light Railway first, something that cannot happen very often with works of this nature. It excludes, though, the Ffestiniog & Blaenau Railway, the Plynlimon & Hafan Tramway and some of the internal systems — the small number of photographs existing of them have been used often elsewhere and nothing new has come to light for many years. It also excludes the tortuous history of the North Wales Narrow Gauge Railways and the Croesor Tramway, which anyway come within the ambit of the even more tortuous history of the Welsh Highland Railway. For the remainder the photographs concentrate, with some exceptions, on the prewar period, comprising a mixture of 'old ones, new ones, loved ones, neglected ones', as Semprini said so often during his Sunday afternoon serenades on the old Light Programme. Some of you may remember.

## Acknowledgements

This book was Peter Waller's idea and I took it on with some reservations. In the event it has been quite enjoyable and I have no hesitation in thanking David Allan (WHR Ltd), John Allsop, Adrian Gray (Festiniog Railway Archives), David Johnson (Millbrook House, and even now still no relation), John Keylock (WHR Ltd), J. R. Morten, Gwyn Price and Bill Rear, for the access they willingly gave to their photographic collections, or the collections under their control, that has made it work. Their willingness to help and, in some cases, to be deprived of their treasured photographs for several months, has made this a considerably better book. Paul Ingham provided technical advice, for which I am grateful, but is not responsible for any errors I might unwittingly have created or perpetuated.

*Peter Johnson*
Leicester
March 1999

## Note

*Welsh place names*
Over the last 50 years some of the places mentioned within this book have reverted to traditional Welsh spellings. In most cases the archaic form has been retained where it was felt appropriate to the context.

*Left:*
The sight of the narrow gauge train crossing one of the town's main streets was a feature of Welshpool life for just over 50 years but never lost its capacity to attract attention. This view shows the *Countess* in GW livery, before it went to Swindon for rebuilding in 1930.
*Commercial postcard/ Peter Johnson Collection*

*Centre left:*
This postcard view of Golfa station was sufficiently, and maybe surprisingly, popular for it to be reprinted several times. It must rate as one of the oldest photographs taken of the railway and, due to tree growth, is unrepeatable nearly 100 years on.
*Commercial postcard/Dainty Series/Peter Johnson Collection*

*Below left:*
A mixed train at Castle Caereinion in the early years. The guard chats with the engine crew but there is no sign of any passengers; the village the station served is a good stiff walk away.
*Millbrook House Collection*

*Right:*
Llanfair Caereinion c1903, showing an impressive array of uniformed staff. The guard, third from left, has a Bell Punch machine around his neck. A Cambrian Railways poster is exhibited on the notice board.
*WLRPS/Peter Johnson Collection*

# 1. Welshpool & Llanfair Light Railway

The Welshpool & Llanfair Light Railway is unusual among most of those described in this book, in that it had no exported mineral traffic. It is also the only one of 2ft 6in gauge and the first narrow gauge railway built under the auspices of the 1896 Light Railways Act.

There had been several schemes for railways to serve the locality, including one by Brunel, and local demand for a rail connection intensified after the opening of the Oswestry & Newtown Railway, later part of the Cambrian Railways, as far as Pool Quay, Welshpool, in 1860.

An 1877 Act of Parliament authorised a standard gauge railway between Welshpool and Llanfair but it was not built, due to lack of financial support, and was formally abandoned in 1882. A scheme for a narrow gauge line was approved in 1887 but that also failed to gain sufficient support. New legislation, the 1896 Light Railways Act already referred to, was seized upon with alacrity and a Light Railway Order was made in 1899. Construction started in 1901, with nearly 75% of the eventual £56,900 cost being met from the public purse.

Opened in 1903, the Welshpool & Llanfair Light Railway served a lightly populated area to the west of Welshpool, then in the County of Montgomery and since 1974 in the County of Powys, 20 miles west of Shrewsbury. The route, just over nine miles long as built, made crossings of several streams and rivers. These tributaries of the River Severn gave rise to fertile farmland in the valley bottoms and

provided the impetus for the construction of the railway. Agricultural traffic and incoming coal and lime sustained its operation.

In its route the railway became best known for the way in which it crept through Welshpool, emerging from blind alleyways to cross public roads in the centre of the town, for it had a terminus adjacent to the standard gauge station and the Smithfield market. On leaving the town by a crossing of Raven Square, the railway headed westwards, following Sylfaen Brook and climbing, partly at 1 in 29, to a 620ft summit at the pass between Pen-y-foel and Y Golfa, hills of 900 and 1,000ft respectively. It then descended, to pass a roadside halt called Sylfaen, before climbing briefly to gain access to the Meifod Valley at Castle Caereinion. The line again descended, down the valley side, following a tributary of the Banwy to Cyfronydd where the Afon Banwy, itself a feeder of the River Vrnwy, was joined just after crossing another stream by the five-arch Brynelin Viaduct. The Banwy was then crossed by a substantial bridge, from which point the line rose slightly as it ran alongside the river until it reached the terminus on the outskirts of Llanfair Caereinion.

Stations were provided at Castle Caereinion, Cyfronydd, Heniarth and the termini. Apart from Welshpool, the railway was hardly convenient for any of the places served, although passengers as well as goods were carried. Loops at the stations were merely double-ended sidings, wagons being left there for local farmers to load and unload them. Operations were conducted on a 'one engine in steam' basis; in 1907, Castle Caereinion was signalled for the crossing of trains but the facility was rarely used. On opening, the rolling stock included three bogie carriages, 40 open wagons and four four-wheel vans, as well as two Beyer Peacock 0-6-0T locomotives, named *The Earl* and *The Countess* after the Earl and Countess of Powis. The Earl had given land for the railway, as well as being a director and shareholder of the company.

The independent company that had built the railway then contracted out its operation to the

*Left:*
*The Earl* waits to leave Llanfair Caereinion in 1925; notice that the vacuum pipe is not on its dolly, so the train will not be leaving just yet. Although carrying GWR livery and numberplate, the locomotive has yet to visit Swindon for overhaul and equipping with additional brasswork, although the GWR has fitted the steam heat equipment that is prominent on this side.
*A. W. Croughton/
Millbrook House Collection*

*Above right:*
A passenger train in the W&L goods yard, not long before the GWR withdrew the passenger service in 1931. The narrow gauge loco shed is behind the second coach. *Real Photos*

*Centre right:*
A contrasting view of a 1950s goods train.
*Millbrook House Collection*

*Below right:*
A view from the back of the train as it approaches Raven Square in the 1950s. The entrance to the present station is in the field on the right.
*Millbrook House Collection*

*Left:*
A fine portrait of *The Earl* outside Welshpool loco shed on 20 March 1941. Enthusiastic cleaning has nearly erased the GWR's tank-side signwriting. The cylinder cover betrays a close encounter with a trackside object. *J. Gowring/ Millbrook House Collection*

*Below:*
The restricted formation available to the W&L as it passed through the back of the town had to be seen to be believed. *The Earl* passes on washday, 12 October 1951. *F. W. Shuttleworth*

neighbouring Cambrian Railways. It was not to be a profitable arrangement for either party; the owning company was severely undercapitalised and there was never sufficient revenue to cover either dividends or operating costs. However, the Cambrian continued to operate it until 1922, when the Great Western Railway took over operations, later making arrangements to absorb the narrow gauge company.

The basic service of three mixed trains daily was maintained by the GWR but in 1925 a road passenger service commenced under railway auspices. There was already road competition in the area so the GWR decided that if the populace wanted to travel by road, it was best that it did so in railway-owned vehicles! The railway passenger service continued until 1931 when it was withdrawn as an economy measure; by so doing, the line could be operated by one shift of staff instead of two. The end of the passenger service also made it possible to reduce track maintenance. Expenses were not exactly reduced to a minimum, for

both locomotives were reboiled and 'Swindonised' in 1929. The GWR also renumbered the locomotives as Nos 822/3, fixing standard Great Western cast numberplates to the tank sides; the nameplates thus displaced were removed to the cab sidesheets, that of *The Countess* (No 823) being abbreviated to *Countess* in the process.

To look forward, the railway was nationalised in 1948 and continued to be operated by British Railways until 1956. Operation as a preserved line commenced in 1963, with restoration of the route between Llanfair Caereinion and Welshpool (Raven Square) completed in 1981.

*Below:*
A little further along the train is slightly further away from the houses. *The Earl* on 12 October 1951.
*F. W. Shuttleworth*

*Above left:*
The Earl approaches Raven Square on 12 October 1951. *F. W. Shuttleworth*

*Below left:*
Heniarth station, one of the line's intermediate stations that served, in this case, an extremely small community; 12 October 1951. *F. W. Shuttleworth*

*Above:*
The end of the line (1) —*The Earl* at Llanfair Caereinion on 12 October 1951. *F. W. Shuttleworth*

*Right:*
The end of the line (2) — the last train under British Railways' auspices but it proved not to be the last train ever. *Millbrook House Collection*

*Left:*
Devil's Bridge on a busy day c1911. 2-6-2T No 2 *Prince of Wales* waits to leave for Aberystwyth. The train just arrived has a locally-modified open coach at the rear.
*J. Valentine*

*Centre left:*
On a murky, and cooler, day a similar scene is seen. Again, the open carriage on the train just arrived is a local conversion, this time from a timber wagon. (During the winter it reverted to its intended purpose.) There is no sign of it being equipped with either continuous brakes or through piping.
*Millbrook House Collection*

*Below left:*
A Devil's Bridge-bound train crossing Park Avenue in the 1960s. Trains ceased to pass this way at the end of the 1967 season.
*Millbrook House Collection*

*Right:*
2-6-2T No 7 *Owain Glyndwr* and train pass the original VoR loco shed, left, in the 1960s.
*Millbrook House Collection*

# 2. Vale of Rheidol Light Railway

In that it was built by a private company, operated by the Cambrian Railways, Great Western Railway and British Railways, the Vale of Rheidol Light Railway has much in common with the Welshpool & Llanfair Light Railway. However, the VoR was simultaneously the last narrow gauge railway and the last steam railway operated by British Railways. In a changed environment it was arguably the first part of the national network to be privatised.

At the end of the 19th century the Rheidol Valley, near Aberystwyth, was a hive of industrial activity. The various metal mines in the area were in increasing need of improved communications between them and the port and growing resort of Aberystwyth. The

Manchester & Milford Railway had obtained powers to build a standard gauge line to Devil's Bridge, at the head of the valley, in 1861 but the scheme did not come to fruition.

The miners, and others, had to continue using the poor quality road network with pack animals until 1902, when the 1ft 11½ in gauge Vale of Rheidol Light Railway was opened to traffic. In the 11¾ miles from Aberystwyth to Devil's Bridge the line climbs 680ft, 480ft of this being achieved on a gradient of 1 in 50 over the last four miles from Aberffrwd. As might be imagined, the route sticks closely to the contours in a way that no standard gauge line ever could, demonstrating the constructional value of building narrow gauge lines in mountainous districts.

To build the railway the contractor used equipment, including a 2-4-0T Bagnall locomotive, from the nearby and then recently closed Plynlimon & Hafan Railway. The VoR took over the engine and wagons when construction was finished, naming the engine *Rheidol*. It was scrapped by the GWR in 1924 but some of the Plynlimon & Hafan wagons survived and remain in use. To work alongside the Bagnall, the company purchased two 2-6-2T locomotives built to its requirements by Davies & Metcalfe of Romiley. They were the only locomotives ever built by this company. The VoR named them *Edward VII* and *Prince of Wales*.

The new railway traded with a modicum of success, small profits being made each year. In 1910 control of the line passed to nominee directors of the Cambrian Railways and in 1913 that company took over the narrow gauge company. In 1912 traffic was so heavy that an engine, *Palmerston*, was borrowed from the Festiniog Railway.

The new management did not appear to devote the same attention to the Rheidol line as its original owners did and the railway entered a period of gradual decline. It was still necessary, however, to borrow the FR's *Palmerston* in 1913 and 1914, an arrangement terminated only by the outbreak of war.

Mining in the Rheidol Valley had been in decline since the railway opened and after World War 1 ended several of the mines closed, reducing still further the small amount of mineral traffic carried by rail. Passenger traffic did increase though, especially in the summer months, and it was necessary to borrow *Palmerston* again in 1921 and 1922.

The Cambrian was then itself absorbed by the Great Western Railway in 1923 and a review of services was undertaken. Two locomotives were built at Swindon in 1923 to designs based on those of Davies & Metcalfe and in 1924 a third was erected, using the spare parts made the previous year for the first two! For many years it was said, by the GWR

originally, that the third Swindon-built locomotive, now No 9, was a rebuild of one of the Davies & Metcalfe machines. The reason for the deception was to fool the GWR's accountants, as construction of three new locomotives would not have been sanctioned, although they were considered necessary. The Bagnall and one of the Davies & Metcalfe locomotives were scrapped in 1924, the second D&M locomotive meeting the same fate in 1935.

Further activities under GWR ownership included closing the Harbour branch, providing four open carriages in 1923, moving the Aberystwyth terminus to a site alongside the main line station in 1924 and replacing the original carriages in 1938. In 1923 two cattle vans were supplied but so little use was found for them, it being said that there were no cattle in the valley, that in 1937 they were regauged and sent to the Welshpool & Llanfair Light Railway. By the end of the 1920s the goods traffic had gone completely and in 1931 the winter service was withdrawn. The Vale of Rheidol Light Railway had become exclusively a tourist line.

In 1939 the railway was closed for the duration of World War 2. Services were resumed in 1945, a prompt restoration being aided by the occasional maintenance attention given to the stock and track during the closure. Ownership was transferred to the Brecon Mountain Railway Ltd in 1989, following which a considerable investment has been made in the railway.

*Above:*
Passing the Erwtomau mine on a horseshoe curve 9½ miles from Aberystwyth, probably early 1950s.
*D. Constance*

*Below:*
An unusual day at Devil's Bridge in 1938, when all three locomotives are in the station. White carriage roofs betray the identity of carriages newly delivered from Swindon. *H. F. Wheeller/ Millbrook House Collection*

*Above:*
A very plain-looking 2-6-2T No 9, built at Swindon in 1924, about to leave Devil's Bridge on 16 August 1952. *F. W. Shuttleworth*

*Below:*
An interesting view of a Rheidol tank in the mighty Swindon Works. The inscription on the back of this photograph claims to show No 8 there in the early 1930s but it had only left there in 1923, brand new! Even if it needed boiler work it should not have required attention to its tanks, as apparently shown, and No 8 was built with tank-side hand rails, but No 7 did not have them fitted until later.
*Stanley J. Rhodes/Millbrook House Collection*

# 3. Corris Railway

The Corris Railway shared with the Welshpool & Llanfair Light Railway and the Vale of Rheidol Light Railway, operation by the Great Western Railway and British Railways. Regrettably the latter found an excuse to close the line very shortly after taking it over on nationalisation in 1948. At 2ft 3in the line's gauge is shared with the nearby Talyllyn Railway, just as the quarries that the railways served shared the same slate veins.

Authorised by the 1858 Corris, Machynlleth & River Dovey Tramroad Act, the 11-mile-long Corris Railway opened in 1859. It served quarries north of the market town of

Machynlleth, primarily at Upper Corris and at Aberllefenni. In doing so it provided an outlet to wharfs on the banks of the Afon Dyfi at Derwenlas, although very little traffic passed to these wharfs after the completion of the standard gauge to Borth in 1863.

As might be expected from the date of its construction, the line was originally horse-worked. A second Act, obtained in 1864, authorised the use of steam traction as well as abandonment of the Machynlleth-Derwenlas section, construction of extensions (that were never built), and change of name to the simpler Corris Railway.

*Left:*
At Corris the railway and the road cross the Afon Deri, a tributary of the Afon Dulas, close together, as shown here, with one of the Hughes tanks on the railway bridge.
*Millbrook House Collection*

The Imperial Tramways Co, of Bristol, purchased the railway in 1878 and ordered three steam locomotives from Hughes Locomotive & Tramway Engineering Works Ltd of Loughborough, later to become the Brush Co. The locomotives were 0-4-0STs, being rebuilt in the first years of the 20th century as 0-4-2STs. The Upper Corris branch, which diverged from the main line at Maespoeth Junction, site of the railway's loco shed, remained horse-worked, as did the line beyond Aberllefenni, where tramways to several quarries joined it. Approval for carriage of passengers was obtained by an Act of 1883, although there is evidence that they had been carried unofficially for many years before; passenger trains operated between Machynlleth and Aberllefenni, 6½ miles. The first carriages were lightweight four-wheelers, almost street tramcars. Their bodies were mounted, two each, on to bogie underframes obtained in 1894, the modifications being carried out by railway personnel. The railway's first bogie coach had been obtained in 1890, with three more following by 1898.

With two of the original locomotives being in poor condition after World War 1, a fourth locomotive, a Kerr Stewart 0-4-2ST, a modern version of the originals, was bought in 1921. The GWR bought the Tramways Company, by then also a bus operator, in 1930 and with it the Corris Railway, almost by accident and certainly not by design! In common with its practice with many of its other branches, the GWR withdrew the passenger service in 1931.

The Corris Railway was closed within five months of being taken over by British Railways in 1948, although the Upper Corris branch, serving Braich Goch and other quarries, had been lifted for wartime salvage from 1941. The final closure was brought about by the threatened scouring of a pier of the Dyfi river bridge near Machynlleth. In the event the bridge situation never worsened but British Railways ensured the line could not be reopened by commencing demolition before the year's end! The two remaining locomotives and some stock were eventually bought for the Talyllyn Railway. A society has been working to reopen a section of the Corris Railway since the 1960s.

*Above:*
No 3 with passenger stock at Aberllefenni in August 1930. With its unique design of bogie coach the Corris Railway tried to recreate the effect of placing two four-wheel bodies on a single underframe, which it had done for its first venture into bogie coach development. The coach with the clerestory, itself a conversion, was apparently much preferred by passengers, for its increased headroom.
*R. G. Jarvis/Millbrook House Collection*

*Below:*
The same train waiting to return to Machynlleth, showing the detail of No 3's rear cab-sheet. Aberllefenni was the limit of locomotive working. There was a horse-worked private tramway serving the Cymerau and Ratgoed Quarries beyond. The clean line of No 3's bufferbeam does raise questions about the use of continuous brakes on the uphill journey! The locomotive is stopped in forward gear.
*R. G. Jarvis/Millbrook House Collection*

*Left:*
No 4 and passenger stock at Aberllefenni on 9 June 1925. Although the loco was still fairly new, it appears to have sustained some damage to its chimney. *A. W. Croughton/ Millbrook House Collection*

*Centre left:*
The first Dyfi river bridge. If a three-coach train with no passengers was not typical, then the photograph surely demonstrates that there is nothing new in photographers' special trains.
*Millbrook House Collection*

*Below:*
The second river bridge looking very new, c1907. The train is perhaps more typical and does have passengers, including two riding on the wagon. It was scouring of the left-hand abutment threatening to undermine it that brought about the railway's closure in 1948.
*Millbrook House Collection*

*Right:*
No 3 at Machynlleth in the 1930s. The GWR might not have declared its ownership of the Corris locomotive fleet but it did declare its ownership of some of the wagons.
*H. M. Comber/*
*Festiniog Railway Archives*

*Centre right:*
No 2 had not been used for some time when photographed at Machynlleth on 16 April 1927 — its smokebox door is missing! Its positioning next to the coach, to make a train, is likely to have been the result of the photographer's persuasive powers. Before the year was out further parts had been removed for reuse on No 3, then receiving attention at Maespoeth. No 2 was scrapped in 1930. *Ifor Higgon/*
*Millbrook House Collection*

*Below right:*
After closure in 1948 the surviving Corris locos were unofficially put into 'store' at Machynlleth. In 1951 they were bought for the Talyllyn Railway.
*P. M. Alexander/*
*Millbrook House Collection*

*Left:*
A portrait of No 2 *Dolgoch* at Wharf station. The cab interior detail is of interest, as is the lightweight nature of the homemade cab.
*Peter Johnson Collection*

*Centre left:*
A typical enthusiast's view of a TR train at Wharf, on this occasion showing *Dolgoch*, with 'shed' door, and a short passenger train.
*Peter Johnson Collection*

*Below left:*
*Dolgoch* and train wait to leave with a good number of tourists in the 1930s. The Lancaster carriage is second from the loco. *Millbrook House Collection*

*Right:*
Very likely the first photograph taken of the Talyllyn Railway, showing No 1 without cab and the Brown Marshall coaches at Dolgoch. As the train is stopped and there are passengers on board, there is clearly nothing new about stopping public trains for photographic purposes! The van is in its original form, with a semi-open balcony on the uphill end.
*National Library of Wales*

# 4. Talyllyn Railway

The Talyllyn Railway's similarity of gauge with the Corris Railway has already been noted. It was, however, most noted for scraping through to 1951 with substantially the same stock that had been used to equip the line in 1866. For many years its bucolic atmosphere, of occasional, archaic trains running along rails hidden in the grass, attracted admiration from the cognoscenti. In 1951 it became the first railway to be preserved and run by volunteers, a story that is beyond the scope of this book.

At 2ft 3in gauge, the Talyllyn Railway was opened in 1866, authorised by an Act obtained the year previously, although very likely construction had started before the Act received Royal assent. Including branches it was about 10 miles long and was designed to carry slate from the Bryn Eglwys Quarries to a wharf adjacent to the Cambrian Railways' coast line at Towyn, in the old County of Merioneth. The railway company was a wholly owned subsidiary of the Aberdovey Slate Co, then recently formed to quarry the slate as a diversion from the depressed Manchester cotton trade, itself affected by the American Civil War. It was originally proposed that the railway should terminate at Aberdovey, to take advantage of the harbour there, but construction of the Cambrian Coast line caused these plans to be modified. The route was

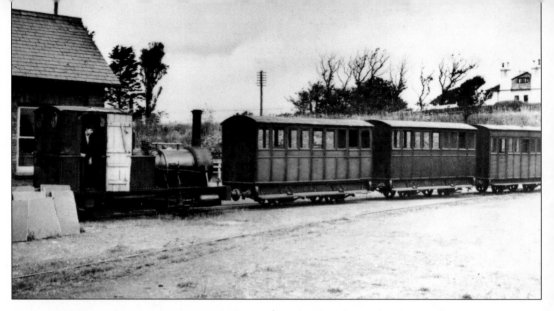

surveyed by James Swinton Spooner, son of James Spooner to whose survey the Festiniog Railway had been built. James Swinton Spooner was also the railway's engineer during construction. The railway is thought to have taken its name from the parish in which its traffic source and eastern terminus were situated; a lake bearing the same name is located three miles to the east of the station.

The line runs along the southern valley side of the Afon Fathew, opposite the mass of the Cader Idris range. The statutory Talyllyn Railway terminated at Abergynolwyn station, some half a mile from the village whose name it bears; access to the quarries was by a branch line three-quarters of a mile long, which made an end-on connection to the main line, and a series of inclines.

On opening the minimum of equipment was provided: two locomotives called *Talyllyn* and *Dolgoch*, four four-wheel carriages, a van and a fleet of wagons. Against the odds, perhaps, this stock sufficed for the Talyllyn Railway for over 80 years. Fletcher Jennings of Whitehaven built the locomotives, *Talyllyn* as an 0-4-0ST in 1864 and *Dolgoch* as an 0-4-0WT in 1866. After some limited use, during which the locomotive was found to be slightly unstable, *Talyllyn* was returned to Whitehaven for modification, returning to Towyn in 1867 as an 0-4-2ST. Both locomotives were delivered without cabs, and had them fitted later by the railway. Brown, Marshall & Co built three carriages and the van and the Lancaster Wagon Co the fourth

carriage. No explanation for the use of a different supplier has been handed down.

Wharf station, the coastal terminus, and a quarter of a mile from the standard gauge station, was for goods only, passengers being accommodated at Pendre, on the edge of the town. Pendre was also the location of the railway's depot and works. The main intermediate station became Dolgoch, where a locomotive water supply was laid on, and close to a fine three-arch viaduct, 62ft high and the line's only major structure, by which it crossed a ravine. The nearby falls are a continuing attraction for visitors. Until 1976 Abergynolwyn, 6¾ miles from Wharf, was the inland passenger terminus. Goods traffic did reach the village by rail, however, as a branch off the mineral line, which included a cable-worked incline, served a goods shed, a sawmill, the Railway Hotel and two terraces of houses.

For most of its existence the Talyllyn Railway was not overladen. Two return trips on six days a week were usually sufficient for the traffic offering, with most trains running mixed. Those few outsiders who came across the line soon decided that it had a charm all its own, especially when they found that the carriages only had doors on one side and that the brake van came with a fully equipped booking office!

The local MP, Sir Henry Haydn Jones, took over the quarries and the railway in 1911 and managed to keep the railway going until he died on 2 July 1950; his executors ran it until the end

of that season. (The remaining working quarry had closed after the roof collapsed in 1946.) As the railway had been run on a shoe-string for so many years, it had become very run down; to many visitors it seemed that the track was only held together by the grass through which it ran!

It seemed likely that the only future for the Talyllyn Railway could be closure.

In 1950 there were no preserved railways and the idea of amateurs involving themselves in railway operation was completely alien, both to enthusiasts and the public. Already, attempts to reopen the Festiniog Railway (closed in 1946) with the aid of volunteers had been unsuccessful.

However, following Sir Henry's death a meeting of enthusiasts was held in Birmingham to consider the matter of the Talyllyn. It was decided to form a preservation society and to approach the executors of the Haydn Jones estate. Following negotiations it was agreed to form a new company to hold the TR's shares, in which both parties would be represented. In this way the first preservation society was formed and with its support the Talyllyn Railway reopened for business in 1951. L. T. C. Rolt, who had called the Birmingham meeting, was appointed to manage the railway; his account of his experiences in 1951 and 1952, entitled *Railway Adventure*, is a classic of railway literature.

*Left:*
*Talyllyn*, also with 'shed' door, waiting to leave Tywyn. This locomotive only ever had a single sandbox on the front running board; a second has been manufactured since preservation. *H. Barton/ Gwyn Price Collection*

*Above:*
A mixed train passing through Pendre yard in 1908. The heavily padlocked wagon-mounted container on the right reveals the likely presence of gunpowder. *G. M. Perkins/ Millbrook House Collection*

*Left:*
Another cheerful party off for a day in the hills.
*Commercial postcard/ Gwyn Price Collection*

*Right:*
*Talyllyn* with a mixed train at Dolgoch in 1949. The photographer's friends are leaning out of the carriage and, judging by the tools lying around, he has cleared the railway's employees out of view. *W. A. Camwell/ Millbrook House Collection*

*Centre right:*
There are plenty of 'real' people in this 1925 view of *Dolgoch* at Dolgoch. *Millbrook House Collection*

*Below:*
Leaving Dolgoch with a mixed train. On this occasion the wagons contain a mixture of tourists and workmen. *Millbrook House Collection*

*Above:*
*Talyllyn* shunts at Nant Gwernol in 1941; the incline to the quarry is off to the left. The photograph shows a braked and an unbraked wagon. *W. A. Camwell/ Millbrook House Collection*

*Right:*
A train of wagons being shunted by *Dolgoch* at Nant Gwernol, c1908. The wagon next to the loco was normally used on the Abergynolwyn village incline for removing night soil from the village. It looks as though another use has been found for it on this occasion — presumably the driver would not have it next to the loco if it had not been well washed out! The second slate wagon is a different type from the remainder. *G. M. Perkins/ Millbrook House Collection*

*Left:*
This picture of the horse tram at Barmouth Ferry was recorded in the publisher's registers in 1912. On the postcard's reverse has been written, regrettably without a date: 'This is our only horse tram. We ferry across to Fairbourne and are taken right round to the village for 1d. It is an old Manchester tram and has been here for 13 years.'
Commercial postcard/ J. Valentine

*Centre left:*
The first steam railway terminus, photographed c1917, with Bassett-Lowke 4-4-2 *Prince Edward of Wales*.
Commercial postcard/J. Valentine

*Below left:*
Bassett-Lowke 4-4-2 *Count Louis* leaving the original Fairbourne station in 1932.
Commercial postcard/J. Valentine

*Right:*
Following a storm in 1927, when Fairbourne was flooded to a depth of 5ft, the line was moved on to a new alignment to the east, more sheltered, side of Penrhyn Point and terminated close to the location of the present car park. There was no loop; the coaches were shunted past the loco by hand. *Count Louis* is shown there in 1932. The line was extended again in 1936.
Commercial postcard/J. Valentine

# 5. Fairbourne Railway

One of the smallest railways covered in this book, the Fairbourne Railway has as long and as varied a history as many of the other lines herein described. Despite its short length and miniature appearance, it does serve a valuable public transport function.

The two mile long Fairbourne Railway started life as a 2ft gauge horse tramway in the 1890s. It was built to aid the development of Fairbourne as a seaside resort, intended to compete with nearby Barmouth. Much of the development was undertaken by McDougall of 'self raising' flour fame. The tramway followed the old road to Penrhyn Point, the embarkation point for ferries across the Mawddach estuary to Barmouth.

As the housing became available for occupation, passenger cars were introduced on the tramway; it ceased to carry materials when building finished. In 1916 the line was taken over by Narrow Gauge Railways Ltd who, in conjunction with Bassett-Lowke, the Northampton model builder, converted it to 15in gauge and introduced steam traction. Narrow Gauge Railways Ltd owned the Ravenglass & Eskdale Railway and the company's proprietors had earlier developed the Rhyl Marine Lake Miniature Railway. The steam locomotive used was 4-4-2 *Prince Edward of Wales*. Designed by Henry Greenly, it had been built by Bassett-Lowke Ltd in 1915.

In 1922 operation was transferred to the Barmouth Motor Boat & Ferry Co, a consortium of local businessmen and ferry boatmen, the latter particularly wishing to protect their commercial interests. This company was not

well run and was in 1924 taken over by the Fairbourne Estate Ltd, the landowner, in lieu of debt. *Prince Edward of Wales* was taken over by the Motor Boat company on lease but in 1923 was sold to the Llewellyn Miniature Railway in Southport. Sir Arthur Heywood's 0-4-0T *Katie*, purchased for £100, replaced it. Built for the Duke of Westminster's Eaton Railway in 1896, *Katie* was worn out by the time it arrived at Fairbourne and was not suitable for the traffic conditions offering; it survived only until 1926. In 1925 *Katie* had, however, been joined by 4-4-2 *Count Louis*. This was another Greenly-designed machine built by Bassett-Lowke. Its construction had been started in 1914 but not completed because of the War. In 1924 it was completed and sold to Count Louis Zborowski, a motor racing driver who unfortunately died before he could take delivery of it. At Fairbourne it was given his name and for 60 years became synonymous with the railway.

From 1926 an oddity was operated at Fairbourne, in the form of an 18in gauge model of a 4-2-2 Stirling 'Single'. The locomotive had been built at Regent Street Polytechnic, London, in 1896. Arguably it was even less suitable for

Fairbourne conditions than *Katie*. A third rail was laid along part of the line to allow it to operate but it was sold in 1936.

After World War 2 the Fairbourne Railway was in a severely damaged state and unfit for use. The Fairbourne Estate Ltd sold it to John Wilkins, owner of the Servis washing machine company. He had the line rebuilt, managing to reopen it throughout in 1947. In the 1950s and 1960s increasing passenger traffic encouraged a considerable investment in new locomotives and rolling stock.

In 1984 the railway changed hands again, bringing major changes to the line, chief among which was the re-gauging of the track to 12¼ in gauge.

*Below:*
*Count Louis* crossing the railway's single civil engineering feature, a bridge across a tidal gully, c1950. At some stage the locomotive had been turned. The first three coaches were built for the railway, in Birmingham, in 1948.
*Commercial postcard/Peter Johnson Collection*

# 6. Festiniog Railway

The Festiniog Railway has a number of claims to greatness. In 1836 it was the first public narrow gauge railway to be built in Britain. In 1869 it successfully introduced the Fairlie locomotive as a means of increasing capacity. In 1872 the first British bogie coaches were built for it. James Spooner's imaginative design for the route allowed loaded slate trains to be run without locomotives, even before steam locomotives could be made small enough for its 2ft gauge. Its history has given rise to consideration being given to designating the railway as a World Heritage Site.

The Festiniog Railway Company gained its Act of incorporation in 1832 and opened its line between Portmadoc and Blaenau Ffestiniog in 1836. Its route had been surveyed by James Spooner and was designed to have a continuous falling gradient down to the harbour, so that laden trains could be worked down by gravity. It was built to carry slate from the quarries at Blaenau Ffestiniog to the harbour at Portmadoc — including the branches to Dinas and Duffws at Blaenau, a distance of just over 14 miles. It was intended that horses would pull the empty wagons back up the hill. A narrow gauge of 1ft 11½ in was adopted, probably because wagons of that gauge were already used within the quarries. The last mile to Portmadoc utilised Madocks's 1811 embankment across the Glaslyn Estuary.

Adapting the continuous gradient to the contours put the railway on to some very

## Portmadoc

*Below:* An unnaturally quiet scene on 6 June 1937, as double Fairlie *Taliesin* waits for departure. *Gwyn Price Collection*

*Left:*
A more natural scene, in August 1939, has the driver rummaging in the toolbox and the fireman checking round his footplate. The blower is on and steam is leaking past the whistle valve. *P. B. Whitehouse/ Millbrook House Collection*

*Centre left:*
The Baldwin was bought for the Welsh Highland Railway in 1923. Its positioning in Harbour station emphasises the curve's super-elevation.
*Millbrook House Collection*

*Below left:*
*Welsh Pony* in September 1933. *G. H. Platt/Bill Rear Collection*

*Right:*
Summer peak service in 1936. *Taliesin's* departure for Blaenau Ffestiniog will be followed by the Baldwin's for the Welsh Highland Railway.
*Millbrook House Collection*

exposed ledges and also resulted in numerous curves. The sharpest of these, called Tyler's after the Board of Trade inspector, is 2½ chains radius. Where the contours were unsuitable, some imposing dry-stone embankments were built; the highest, at Cei Mawr, is 62ft high. To improve the route the Moelwyn Tunnel (730yd) was opened in 1842, followed by the Garnedd Tunnel (60yd) in 1851. The length and narrow bore of the former, combined with a lack of ventilation, were to result in the railway achieving a certain notoriety, especially when the 20th Century's inter-war years brought an increasing number of tourists as passengers.

The demand for slate in the developing industrial areas of England and elsewhere brought much traffic to the railway which was soon operating to capacity. To overcome the difficulties encountered, the track was modernised and in 1863 steam locomotives were introduced. Initially there were four 0-4-0 tank engines built by George England in London; the first batch were named *The Princess, The Prince, Mountaineer* and *Palmerston*. They were followed in 1867 by two similar, but larger, locomotives from the same source, named *Welsh Pony* and *Little Giant*. Only

*Mountaineer* and *Little Giant* have not survived. The others have, over the years, been greatly rebuilt and modified, and *Prince* and *Palmerston* are presently in working order.

The introduction of steam engines led the way to the (official) carriage of passengers, a move that was encouraged by the threat of competing routes to Blaenau Ffestiniog. Using eight tiny four-wheeled carriages built by Brown, Marshall & Co in Birmingham, the first passenger trains ran in 1865. A further six four-wheelers were obtained from Ashbury Railway Carriage & Iron Co in 1868. The running gear for all this stock was built at Boston Lodge.

Increasing traffic again brought operating problems which the company sought to solve by laying a second track. Parliamentary powers had been obtained in 1869 and the necessary land purchases put in hand when the problem was solved by the introduction of a locomotive capable of prodigious feats of haulage when compared with the existing fleet.

The saviour was *Little Wonder*, an articulated locomotive built, also by George England, to Robert Fairlie's patent; Fairlie was married to England's daughter. Delivered in 1869, *Little Wonder* was fitted with a double-ended boiler unit having twin fireboxes in the middle. The

boiler was carried on two four-coupled power bogies which could swivel under it, the crew being carried one on either side of the fireboxes. The resulting machine was effectively twice the size of the original engines but, being articulated, was still able to cope with the railway's bends and gradients. *Little Wonder* proved to be very successful, attracting attention from all over the world. As a mark of gratitude the inventor gave the company free use of the patent and the double Fairlie became the Festiniog's trademark.

Having proved that articulation worked on a locomotive, the company then applied the same principle to its passenger stock in a move to increase both capacity and comfort. 1872 saw the introduction of two iron-framed bogie carriages, most likely the first of this type to run in the British Isles. Also built by Brown Marshalls, these vehicles, Nos 15 and 16, have survived in traffic; at the time of publication they are about to undergo a major overhaul with the benefit of Lottery funding. Brown Marshalls delivered two more bogie coaches, developments of the 1872 pair, in 1876 and in 1879 the Gloucester Wagon Co delivered a further similar pair. Ashbury delivered the final new 19th Century passenger carriages to the FR in 1897 and 1898. They were more basic vehicles, with a capacity of 56 passengers each compared to 32-48 in the earlier builds.

Accompanying the bogie coaches were three bogie luggage/brake vans built by Brown Marshalls in 1873 (two) and 1876. Their distinctive roofline has attached to them the soubriquet 'curly roof van' in modern FR parlance. One of them was rebuilt with two passenger compartments and a roof of more normal appearance in 1921. Two further bogie vans, with normal roofs, were obtained from Brown Marshalls in 1880. The railway also used in passenger trains a number of four-wheeled vans, some braked, that were made at Boston Lodge.

For its quarrymen passengers the Festiniog Railway supplied some of the most basic carriages ever built. The first ones, introduced around 1867, had neither roofs nor doors. Later versions were roofed but doorless, the older ones being modified to match. From 1885 new quarrymen's carriages had doors, glazed windows and roofs, all mod cons — but they were still very basic carriages.

Of immeasurably more significance to the FR than the passenger stock was the freight stock. The railway eventually had over 1,000 slate wagons, each capable of carrying a two-ton load. Most were built at Boston Lodge except for one batch built by Brown Marshalls. These included some three-ton wagons, intended to increase capacity, but they proved difficult to load and were not repeated. The railway had

*Continued on page 44.*

## Boston Lodge

*Above:*
A very cluttered view of the erecting shop in 1933, with *Palmerston's* boiler after the centre-ring from *Little Giant's* boiler had been riveted in. The locomotive's frames are to the left and its tank obscured by the smokebox. *H. W. Comber/ Festiniog Railway Archives*

*Below:* Inside the loco shed, also in 1933, 1872-built *James Spooner* has been dismantled, its boiler resting on timber baulks and planks supported on barrels — one doubts if the breaking strain of these was ever calculated! In the foreground is a power bogie, the locomotive's tanks/bunkers are alongside the walls. At the rear are *Princess* and another England locomotive. *H. W. Comber/Festiniog Railway Archives*

*Left:*
*Merddin Emrys* and crew pose outside the loco shed. The coal in *Merddin's* bunkers does not appear to have much substance to it. *A. W. Croughton/ Millbrook House Collection*

*Centre left:*
*Taliesin,* formerly *Livingston Thompson,* and crew in the 1930s. *H. W. Comber/ Festiniog Railway Archives*

*Below left:*
The WHR Baldwin at Boston Lodge loco shed for coaling. This was almost the limit of working for this loco on the FR; there is evidence that suggests it must have been turned on the turntable located on the far side of the shed at least once. *Millbrook House Collection*

*Above right:*
In the 1930s Glan-y-mor yard became known for being a repository for bits of dismantled locomotives. In this 1933 view are the cabs of *James Spooner* and *Taliesin* (the single Fairlie) and *Little Giant's* saddle tank. *H. W. Comber/ Festiniog Railway Archives*

*Right:*
Also in 1933, the tanks and chassis of *Taliesin* were still to be seen. The previous year the locomotive's name had been transferred to double Fairlie *Livingston Thompson.* *H. W. Comber/ Festiniog Railway Archives*

many other goods and service wagons, a few converted from slate wagons. A small fleet of gunpowder vans were the only private-owner wagons to operate on the railway. A vehicle unique to the narrow gauge was the hearse van, converted from a quarrymen's coach. Hidden away at Blaenau Ffestiniog, where it escaped the attention of visiting railway enthusiasts, until the closure, it can have seen very little use but it did survive to become a museum exhibit.

Having proved the capabilities of the Fairlie locomotive and its suitability for the line, a second was ordered, and delivered in 1872. Named *James Spooner*, it was designed by George Percival Spooner and built by the Avonside Engine Co in Bristol. In 1876 the railway took delivery of a single Fairlie, effectively half a *James Spooner*. Also designed by George Percival Spooner, it was built by the Vulcan Foundry and named *Taliesin*. It had many similarities with the six-coupled locomotives from the same designer, supplied to the North Wales Narrow Gauge Railways by

## Tan-y-bwlch

*Above:*
Contrasting views from the old footbridge — a cabless *Little Giant* facing downhill in the 1880s. The train is without continuous brakes at this time. *F. Bedford/Millbrook House Collection*

*Above right:*
The single Fairlie *Taliesin* with a down passenger crossing an up mixed. *F. Bedford/ Millbrook House Collection*

*Right:*
*Prince*, like *Little Giant* also facing downhill, after the passengers' waiting shelter has been replaced by the cottage. By this time the station building is equipped with vending machines as well as advertising. The last vehicle in the train is an Ashbury four-wheeler, a type that does not survive. *Millbrook House Collection*

the same maker the year before. Both these locomotives remained in service until the 1930s.

During the last years of the 19th Century the Festiniog Railway reached its peak, culminating in the construction, in 1879 and 1885, of two double engines, *Merddin Emrys* and *Livingston Thompson*, in its own Boston Lodge Works. George Percival Spooner designed these locomotives too. His father, Charles Easton Spooner, had an inventive streak that had helped bring the railway to public attention. In turn, it had been Charles Easton's father, James Spooner, who had surveyed the railway's route and had overseen the completion of its construction. It is no coincidence that the era of the Festiniog Railway's pre-eminence in the field of narrow gauge railways coincided with the period in which the Spooners were involved with the railway. Charles Easton Spooner, and Robert Francis Fairlie, promoted the cause of the narrow gauge, and specifically the Festiniog Railway and the Fairlie patent locomotive, widely. Their influence is to be seen world-wide in many of the narrow gauge railways built during the last quarter of the 19th Century.

With the arrival of the 20th Century the FR was to enter a period of decline which was to end, in 1946, in closure and abandonment. The decline was caused both by the tapping of the Blaenau slate traffic by the LNWR (from 1881) and the GWR (from 1883) and the development of alternative roofing materials. A strike in the quarries in 1913 aggravated the situation, in which dividend payments took priority over maintenance. Followed by the Great War and then the Great Depression, the railway had no chance to catch up with the arrears and the decline hastened.

The only bright spot arose during the 1920s: the number of passengers carried was considerably increased by tourists seeking to view the remote scenic splendours visible from the 'Toy Railway' or 'Faery Line', as the company promoted itself, while they passed through the Vale of Ffestiniog. Even this traffic was to wane during the 1930s, despite efforts to attract new business. Engine failures could easily make travel on the 'Faery Line' a journey of epic proportions, with missed connections with the standard gauge links commonplace. Meanwhile, the quarrymen took to the buses.

In 1923 the narrow gauge Welsh Highland Railway was opened from Portmadoc to Dinas, near Carnarvon, via Aberglaslyn, a distance of 22 miles. It was never successful and closed on 31 December 1933. The FR took a lease on its neighbour and operated a summer service during the following three years, though with no greater success. At the end of the 1936 season the line was closed for good.

From 1923, until he died in 1931, the railway came under the influence of the light railway king, Col Holman F. Stephens. The Colonel was well known for the ramshackle collection of minor railways he ran, with varying degrees of success, from an office in Tonbridge, Kent. In addition to being a member of the FR Company board, he was also appointed Engineer, Managing Director, Locomotive Superintendent and Company Chairman at various times, sometimes concurrently. Stephens was also involved with the Welsh Highland Railway at the same time. Unfortunately his imperious, rather brusque, approach was not well received by spirited Welsh railwaymen and the two sides agreed rarely, if at all, on the best way of achieving the desired result. Col Stephens was responsible for the purchase of ex-War Department Simplex and Baldwin tractors for shunting use.

The FR's passenger service was withdrawn on the outbreak of war in 1939. Slate trains continued to run as required, and when motive power was available, throughout the war. Afterwards it quickly became clear that there were no resources, either within the railway or elsewhere, to repair the track and rolling stock, so in 1946 the Festiniog Railway was closed.

Powers to close the line legally could only be had by spending money the company did not have to promote an Act of Parliament. Everything was left to rot, or to be vandalised, where it stood.

Almost immediately attempts were made to find ways of reopening the railway, possibly using volunteers to assist a nucleus of paid staff. Eight years were to pass before all the legal and financial obstacles were overcome and a group of people, including Alan Pegler, provider of the necessary financial support, were able to implement a new regime. The newly formed Festiniog Railway Society supported them.

*Right:*
It seems that few camera-toting visitors would pass through Tan-y-bwlch without photographing Bessie Jones. This picture was used as a cigarette card. The train seems exceedingly short; the churns alongside it were used to carry milk from Creuau Farm, behind the station, to a dairy in Blaenau Ffestiniog.
*David Allan Collection*

*Centre right:*
Bessie sold teas from her living room in the station cottage. On a fine day a table has been moved outside to attract customers. *Commercial postcard/E. M. Jones/ Bill Rear Collection*

*Below right:*
In the 1930s, when the carriages are painted different colours, *Taliesin's* water tanks are stained by impurities in the water being used. Bessie works the train, selling picture postcards.
*Millbrook House Collection*

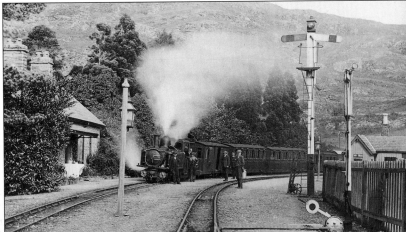

# Blaenau Ffestiniog

*Left:*
*Palmerston* shunting at Glan-y-pwll in the 1930s. The splendid electric headlamp is powered by the battery mounted in front of the sandpot. *H. W. Comber/ Festiniog Railway Archives*

*Centre left:*
*Princess* shunting at Duffws. *Millbrook House Collection*

*Below left:*
*Palmerston* waits to leave Duffws, probably in the last days before the station's closure in 1922. *Real Photos*

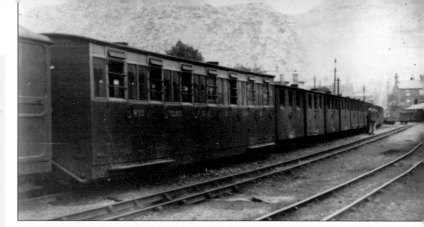

*Right:*
The quarrymen's train at Duffws. Built in 1896 by Ashbury, No 22 was reckoned to be a rough ride and was avoided by regular passengers, hence its relegation to the quarrymen's train! The quarrymen, however, probably found it a considerable improvement on their 1885-built four-wheelers.
*Gwyn Price Collection*

*Centre right:*
Carriages and wagons stabled at Duffws. The hearse van spent most of its years in the shelter behind the water tank.
*Gwyn Price Collection*

*Below:*
Blaenau Ffestiniog GW interchange platform on a fine summer's day in the 1930s. The locomotive is *Taliesin*.
*Millbrook House Collection*

# Back along the line

# 7. Welsh Highland Railway

The story of the Welsh Highland Railway is one of great complexity and one where events invariably turned against the railway's promoters, to the inevitable detriment of the railway. It arose from a desire to link Portmadoc with Carnarvon by narrow gauge railway, to put Beddgelert on the railway map, to open up the Gwyrfai valley and, because Charles Easton Spooner was involved, to create another Festiniog Railway, with the success of that railway.

It grew out of the Croesor Tramway, the North Wales Narrow Gauge Railways (NWNGR); and the Portmadoc, Beddgelert & South Snowdon Railway (PBSSR), these lines all being, or intended to be, 1ft 11½ in gauge.

The Croesor Tramway was a horse tramway that gave the Croesor Valley slate quarries access to Portmadoc. It was built on private land and without Parliamentary approval, opening in 1864; its legal position was regularised by an Act the following year.

The NWNGR was a railway with a main line between Dinas Junction, near Carnarvon, and Rhyd Ddu and a branch to Bryngwyn, in all 12 miles of route called the Moel Tryfan Undertaking. An Act was obtained in 1872, authorising the Moel Tryfan Undertaking and the General Undertaking, the latter linking the Croesor Tramway with Betws-y-coed. The

## The junction railways

*Below:*
The junction railways were built to link the FR to the Welsh Highland Railway in 1923. Barely 10 chains (220yd) long, they were authorised by the FR's 1923 Light Railway Order. In September 1933, judging by the shadows and the dress on the young women on the left apparently an Indian Summer, *Taliesin* stands on the junction railway at its boundary with the statutory (1832) FR.
*G. H. Platt/Millbrook House Collection*

*Left:*
*Merddin Emrys* at the same spot in the 1930s, sandwiched between wagons and carriages. *Millbrook House Collection*

General Undertaking was never built but neither was it forgotten. The NWNGR had Charles Easton Spooner as one of its promoters and the Undertakings mentioned were but fragments of the original NWNGR proposals. The railway was opened in 1878 and the company went into receivership the same year!

The PBSSR was a subsidiary of the North Wales Power & Traction Co (NWPTC), developer of the Cwm Dyli hydro-electric power station. NWPTC apparently thought it would be easier to gain approval for its transmission lines to pass through Snowdonia if it promoted electrically operated narrow gauge railways along the same routes! Therefore the PBSSR intended to connect the NWNGR to the Croesor Tramway, via Beddgelert and the Aberglaslyn Pass, to upgrade part of the Croesor, and to electrify the entire route. It also proposed a route from Beddgelert to Betws-y-coed and Corwen. Between 1901 and 1908 several Acts of Parliament and Light Railway Orders were obtained but only a little work was ever carried out, in the vicinity of Beddgelert around 1906, the remains of which may still be seen. Pursuant of its aims the PBSSR had bought the Croesor Tramway in 1901 but no changes were made to it or to its method of operation.

In 1922 the Welsh Highland Railway Co was created by a Light Railway Order promoted by the Caernarvonshire County Council to take over the NWNGR, which had been moribund since 1916, and the PBSSR, which had ceased trading in 1919, and to restore and complete them as appropriate. The electrification plans were abandoned, requiring a Light Railway Amendment Order to authorise a new route suitable for steam locomotives around Beddgelert. The NWNGR section reopened in 1922. Allied with the WHR development was a junction with the Festiniog Railway at Portmadoc, sanctioned by another Light Railway Order. The FR's Order also approved the construction of a new Portmadoc station owned by the FR and located on the WHR, intended to be used jointly by the two railways. The complete railway was opened in 1923.

*Above right:*
*Welsh Pony's* train has just crossed the Britannia Bridge, returning to the FR from the WHR in the 1930s. The board on the left promotes the Lemon Tub Teashop, 'on right near the end of the High Street'. Under the loco the siding runs on to J. W. Greaves' wharf, the location of the present day station car park. *Millbrook House Collection*

*Right:*
Another sandwich combination. This time the Baldwin is propelling a rake of coal wagons towards the FR while it brings a train off the WHR! The board behind the audience of small boys promotes the location of the Oakeley Wharf. The date is 1936. *E. R. Morten*

## Along the line

*Left:*
*Russell* at Portmadoc New (1929) station in 1932. Standard gauge wagons are visible on the Beddgelert Siding (left).
*H. W. Comber/ Festiniog Railway Archives*

*Below left:*
Smartly painted after the FR lease of the WHR commenced in 1934, Hunslet 2-6-2T *Russell* is seen at Beddgelert.
*Millbrook House Collection*

*Below right:*
A classic scene at Beddgelert when the WHR was very new. All the stock visible belongs to the FR. The loco is *Little Giant*.
*Millbrook House Collection*

The WHR was funded by debenture loans from the local authorities and the Ministry of Transport. The contractor, Alfred McAlpine, accepted part payment in debentures. The issue of ordinary shares was the method of payment for the NWNGR and PBSSR assets. The FR and the WHR had directors in common but they were primarily NWPTC men and strategic direction came from that company's headquarters at Dolgarrog. From 1923 Col Holman Fred Stephens, well known for keeping a collection of semi-moribund light railways afloat, dealt with civil engineering and locomotive matters. Day-to-day management was carried out from Harbour station and Dinas.

The only stock on the WHR was that previously owned by the NWNGR. There were two steam locomotives; *Moel Tryfan*, a NWNGR 0-6-4T single Fairlie built by Vulcan Foundry in 1875 but since 1917 incorporating the frames of the identical *Snowdon Ranger*; and *Russell*, a Hunslet 2-6-2T built for the PBSSR in 1906. An ex-War Department Baldwin 4-6-0PT, No 590, built in 1917, was obtained in 1923 at Col Stephens' behest. The WHR's coaching stock was the surviving NWNGR fleet of 11 bogie vehicles.

The FR junction railway facilitated the transfer of stock and gave the WHR access to Boston Lodge. Through services to run from Blaenau Ffestiniog to Dinas were scheduled, although they did not last long in practice. To allow them to work through the FR's tunnels, the NWNGR carriage roofs were lowered. On the locomotive side *Moel Tryfan* was successfully modified but the same could not be said for *Russell*. Changes were made to the locomotive but it was still unable to pass through the tunnels, and the locomotive's appearance had been ruined too!

The Welsh Highland Railway was not a success and losses on operation were made each year. Quarries were closing down and prospective passengers were exploring the delights of new-fangled motor transport, cars, buses and charabancs. The winter service was quickly withdrawn. Col Stephens was appointed receiver in 1927. When no financial improvement was found to be possible during the following six years the line was closed. In the following year, 1934, it was reopened by the FR under the terms of a 42-year lease. By this time the railway had a reputation for

prolonged journey times and missed connections. Despite attempts to increase traffic, the FR could do no better and it was decided not to operate the line from 1937. The Welsh Highland Railway was abandoned to the elements.

In 1941 the track between Dinas and Croesor Junction was, with locomotives and other material and equipment, requisitioned to aid the war effort. The remainder was left in case the Croesor quarries reopened when hostilities ceased. None of the investing authorities made anything out of the railway and neither did the FR. The Croesor quarries did not reopen after the war and the remaining track, including that of the Croesor Tramway, was lifted by 1950.

Attempts to reinstate the Welsh Highland Railway were first made in the 1960s. As this book was published (June 1999) the news was that permission had been given for reconstruction to commence.

*Left:*
Approaching Rhyd Ddu from Waunfawr with *Russell* at the head of the train.
*W. H. Whitworth*

*Centre left:*
An FR train arrives at Waunfawr, bound for Dinas. The guard looks out for passengers.
*Commercial postcard/R. Tuck*

*Below:*
*Russell* and the Bryngwyn branch goods at Dinas in 1932. The interesting consist includes two of the four ex-WD Hudson bogie wagons bought under Col Stephens's influence in 1925. (The FR bought five of these wagons in 1926, three of which were used by the WHR.) The train also includes Festiniog Railway coal wagons and, at the rear, two NWNGR vans. *H. W. Comber/ Festiniog Railway Archives*

# 8. Nantlle Tramway

The Nantlle Tramway has the significance of being the first public railway in Caernarvonshire. It underwent several changes during its 135 years; a narrow gauge tramway, it was taken over by a standard gauge company and truncated. There were, due to quarrying requirements, changes of route too, yet the surviving section remained horse-worked throughout, finally having the distinction of being operated by British Railways.

An Act of Parliament made in 1825 authorised the incorporation of Nantlle Railway Co and its construction of the Nantlle Tramway. At nine miles long, the 3ft 6in gauge railway was opened in 1828. It ran from the slate quarries in the Nantlle Vale to Carnarvon via Penygroes.

The Tramway was operated with the quarry owners/operators themselves providing their own horses and wagons, paying tolls for its use. There were 22 passing places along the single line. Passengers were carried from 1856, although there is some doubt about the legitimacy of this provision. In addition to the terminals there were stations at Bontnewydd, Pwllheli Road (Llanwnda), Groeslon and

Penygroes. Contractor Thomas Savin took over the tramway in 1866 and it was absorbed into the Carnarvonshire Railway in 1867.

The Carnarvon-Penygroes section, just over 6 miles, became part of the Carnarvonshire Railway's Afon Wen-Carnarvon standard gauge route. To procure an acceptable standard gauge route between Carnarvon and Dinas, several deviations of line and level were made. As a result substantial parts of the original formation between Coed Helen (Caernarfon) and Dinas have survived, including tunnels at Coed Helen and Plas Dinas and the bridge over the Afon Gwyrfai at Bont Newydd, and some can be seen from the new Welsh Highland Railway (Caernarfon).

Following the LNWR takeover of the Carnarvon Railway in 1870, the Nantlle Railway from Penygroes to Talysarn, less than two miles, was converted to standard gauge; it closed in 1963. The remainder of the line remained 3ft 6in gauge and horse-worked and, also being part of British Railways, it too closed in 1963. The Carnarvonshire Railway was closed in 1964. Track was lifted between Dinas and Afon Wen in 1968 and the remainder in 1970.

*Right:*
Loaded wagons under way approaching the exchange sidings at Tal-y-sarn. The double-flanged wagon wheels are evident.
*Millbrook House Collection*

# 9. Padarn Railway

Both its gauge, 4ft, and its method of working, carrying loaded wagons of slate on transporter wagons, made the Padarn Railway unusual. It remained in use until 1961. In more enlightened times public demand might have ensured that more of it survived. As it is, at Llanberis part of its route was adapted to become the Llanberis Lake Railway.

The Padarn Railway was built to convey the output of the Dinorwic Slate Quarries, just outside Llanberis, to the quarry-owned Port Dinorwic on the Menai Straits. It was a 4ft gauge line brought into use in 1843 to replace an earlier 2ft gauge tramway that dated from 1825. Six and a half miles long, it was privately owned and operated and was built without the benefit of Parliamentary powers. Horse-worked at first, locomotives were introduced in 1848 when two 0-4-0s named *Fire Queen* and *Jenny Lind* were obtained from A. Horlock's Northfleet Ironworks in Kent. They were replaced in 1882 and 1886 by two Hunslet 0-6-0Ts. These were named *Dinorwic* and *Pandora*, the latter later being renamed *Amalthfla*. A third Hunslet, *Velinheli*, was added to the fleet in 1895. These

were the largest locomotives built for the Welsh slate quarrying industry. One of the Horlock engines, *Jenny Lind*, was scrapped but *Fire Queen* was put away in a shed at Gilfach Ddu where it remained until 1969; rumour has it that the owner's daughter had an affection for this locomotive! It is now on display at the Penrhyn Castle Museum, Bangor. The Hunslets were scrapped in 1963, after the line was dismantled by a scrap merchant.

Padarn Railway operations were unusual in that the 1ft 10¾in gauge quarry wagons were carried, loaded, to the port on 4ft gauge transporter wagons. The 4ft gauge railway terminated at Penscoins, above Port Dinorwic. There the quarry wagons were unloaded and let down to the harbour by an incline. A separate 1ft 10¾in gauge railway system was established at the port, with its own allocation of locomotives. No public service was offered but from 1895 until 1947 trains were run for the benefit of the quarrymen, using purpose-built rolling stock paid for, by subscription, by the men themselves! (They also paid for *Velinheli* although they did not have exclusive use of it!)

*Left:*
Withdrawn in 1886, *Fire Queen* next emerged into the light of day in December 1969, 83 years later! *D. Rendell/ Millbrook House Collection*

*Right:*
*Dinorwic* was built in 1882 and reboilered in 1923. Photographed at Gilfach Ddu on 26 June 1956, it was still painted an attractive lined red livery. *Brian Hilton/ Millbrook House Collection*

*Left:*
Hunslet delivered *Amalthfla* in November 1886, when it was named *Pandora*. The renaming occurred in 1909. It was reboilered in 1930. Seen on 24 August 1961. *Ken Cooper/Millbrook House Collection*

*Centre left:*
*Velinheli* was supplied in 1895, the last Padarn loco to be delivered and, in 1953, the first to go out of service. *Ken Cooper/Millbrook House Collection*

*Below left:*
*Dinorwic* prepares to leave Penscoins with empties in 1932. The headlamp is rigged for working the quarrymen's train during the hours of darkness. The chimneys of these locos were equipped with Gilfach Ddu spark arresters.
*H. W. Comber/Festiniog Railway Archives*

The Padarn Railway was closed in October 1961, when road transport was introduced; the port lines fell out of use at the same time.

Two miles of the Padarn Railway route from Gilfach Ddu to Pen Llyn were reopened as the Llanberis Lake Railway in 1971/2. The gauge of this line is 1ft 11½in and the three locomotives owned by the operating company are Hunslet 0-4-0STs from the Dinorwic Quarries. The former quarry workshops at Gilfach Ddu are preserved and open to the public as the Welsh Slate Quarrying Museum; ex-Pen-yr-orsedd Quarry Hunslet 0-4-0ST *Una* is to be found there, occasionally in steam.

*Right:*
A loaded train hauled by *Dinorwic* approaches Penscoins on 26 June 1956. Some enthusiast passengers have joined the brakesman on this occasion. *Brian Hilton/Millbrook House Collection*

*Below:*
In August 1952 *Amalthfla* was captured at Brynrefail crossing, close to the present-day terminus of the Llanberis Lake Railway. *Bill Rear*

*Above:*
*Charles*, the first of the classic Hunslet Penrhyn main line 0-4-0s, seen in 1953. Delivered in 1882, there are detail differences when compared with the 1893-built *Blanche* and *Linda*, notably the square cab-front windows and the positioning and size of the sandboxes. *Charles* was named after the son of the 2nd Baron Penrhyn. It was out of service after 1955 and has been at Penrhyn Castle since 1963.
*P. B. Whitehouse/*
*Millbrook House Collection*

*Centre left:*
A contrasting view of *Linda*. The long front overhang that was a feature of this design is clearly seen in this photograph. The locomotive was named after the daughter of the 3rd Baron Penrhyn.
*George Alliez/*
*Gwyn Price Collection*

*Left:*
*Blanche* in portrait mode. Blanche was the wife of the 3rd Baron Penrhyn, the mother of Linda. *LGRP*

# 10. Penrhyn Railway

The Penrhyn Railway was a private line built for the carriage of slate from the Penrhyn Quarries, near Bethesda, down to Port Penrhyn on the Menai Straits. There were two railways that performed this duty. The first, opened in 1801, incorporated part of an earlier line used to carry slate from a mill at Llandegai to the port, first used in 1798. It was about a mile long with two inclines; the section between the mill and the main line, including an incline, remained in use until 1831. The 1801 line had three inclines along its 6¼ -mile length; it was worked by horse-power and gravity. Following modifications to the route, the first steam locomotive was introduced in 1875; the first locally-built de Winton locomotives were delivered the following year.

A new line, mostly on a new route, superseded the 1801 line in 1879. Seven miles long, it was designed, with the involvement of Charles Easton Spooner, to be locomotive-worked. The gauge was 1ft 10¾ in, the strange measurement probably arising from measuring 2ft across the rails instead of between them. The railway was steam-worked from the start, with de Winton locomotives being used initially. In 1882 the Hunslet 0-4-0ST *Charles* was obtained, followed by the similar *Blanche* and *Linda* in 1893. The names were those of members of the Penrhyn family. These locomotives proved well suited to the line and were in regular use until it closed in 1962. Three World War 1 Baldwin 2-6-2Ts were obtained from a dealer in 1924. Obviously it was expected that they could replace the Hunslets but they were not a success and were abandoned by the end of the 1920s. In 1940 two were scrapped and one exported to Australia. The quarries and the port each had their own separate locomotive allocations, although there was some degree of interchange. Rail use at Port Penrhyn ceased shortly after the main line was closed. As with the Padarn Railway, the only official passengers were the quarrymen; their service finished in 1951.

*Blanche* and *Linda* and a substantial amount of track materials were sold to the Festiniog Railway. Extensively modified and now running as 2-4-0STTs, the locomotives continue to give good service. Most of the track was laid between Tan-y-bwlch and Dduallt, where it is being replaced only as the turn of the century approaches. *Charles* is displayed at Penrhyn Castle Museum.

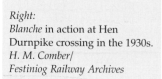

*Right:*
*Blanche* in action at Hen Durnpike crossing in the 1930s.
*H. M. Comber/*
*Festiniog Railway Archives*

*Above:*
*Blanche* receives attention, perhaps to bearings, during steam raising at Port Penrhyn, c1951; a hosepipe has been connected to the injector overflow to keep the workers dry. 1885-built *Winifred* is alongside. *P. B. Whitehouse/ Millbrook House Collection*

*Left:*
With cylinder drain cocks open, *Blanche* moves off shed at Port Penrhyn on 25 June 1956. *Blanche* worked the last train over the PQR in 1962 and was sold to the FR in 1963. *Brian Hilton/ Millbrook House Collection*

*Above:*
A posed picture of *Linda* with wagons. The riveted tank was replaced in 1951. *Linda's* last trip over the PQR was on 11 July 1962; it was delivered to the FR, on loan, three days later. *Gwyn Price Collection*

*Right:*
Baldwin 2-6-2T *Tregarth* had a brief career on the Penrhyn Quarry Railway. It was bought in September 1924, last used in April 1929 and was scrapped in 1940. No photographs have come to light of it, or the other two Baldwins, in use, but several exist of *Tregarth* abandoned at Coed-y-parc; this one dates from the early 1930s. *H. M. Comber/ Festiniog Railway Archives*

## Dinorwic

*Above:*
A tiny part of the Dinorwic system is shown in this photograph, taken on 26 June 1956. *Brian Hilton/ Millbrook House Collection*

*Left:*
*George B*, built in 1898, on the Wellington level in 1958. The loco was named *Wellington* when new. It was sold in 1965. *J. M. Jarvis/ Millbrook House Collection*

# 11. Internal Quarry Systems

## Dinorwic

In the quarries the different levels were served by 1ft 10¾ in gauge railways. Locomotives were used where the length of run or the amount of work warranted it; otherwise manpower was used. Most of the tracks at Port Dinorwic were of this gauge and engines were allocated there for shunting purposes.

From 1870, 29 steam engines and a smaller number of internal combustion locomotives were used at varying times. The steam locomotives were mostly Hunslet 0-4-0ST locomotives of the type that came to be associated with North Wales quarries; the basic design was developed for Dinorwic. The Hunslets had the benefit of one of the most eclectic collection of names to be found anywhere. At first they received the names of members of the Assheton-Smith (quarry owner's) family or quarry locations but then inspiration obviously failed, for seven locomotives were named more prosaically *No 1*,

*No 2* etc. (*No 1*, which has recently been put back into working order on the Bredgar & Wormshill Railway in Kent, was later renamed *Lady Joan* but that lady, the first wife of Sir Charles Michael Duff Bt, allegedly disgraced herself so the more prosaic *No 1* was restored.) Normality was restored, and eclecticism introduced, when a policy of naming, or renaming, the locomotives after winning racehorses in the Assheton-Smith stable commenced. This gave rise to such splendid names as *Cloister*, winner of the 1893 Grand National, *Covert Coat*, winner of the 1913 Grand National, and *Maid Marian*, winner of the 1914

*Below:*
1902-built *Holy War* shunting wagons loaded with small slab in 1952. It was out of use by November 1967 and sold in 1970. Originally named *No 3*, *Holy War* is now owned by the Bala Lake Railway. The short wheelbase and double-flanged wheels on the wagons are worthy of examination.
*P. B. Whitehouse/Millbrook House Collection*

Grand National. Other names used included *Rough Pup*, *Irish Mail* and *Lady Madcap*.

The quarry workshops at Gilfach Ddu were very well equipped, including a substantial foundry, and carried out running repairs to the locomotives; major repairs and rebuilds were carried out at the port by the Port Dinorwic Dry Dock Co, a linked organisation.

The quarries closed in 1969 when the company went into liquidation — much of the site is now that of First Hydro's Dinorwic Power Station, a pumped storage station much larger than the Tanygrisiau prototype which resulted in the Festiniog Railway's deviation being built. While most of the Padarn Railway's equipment was scrapped, this was not to be the fate of the quarry railway's equipment, much of it surviving in Wales and elsewhere.

## Penrhyn

As at Dinorwic the Penrhyn Quarries had extensive rail systems throughout the quarries.

# Penrhyn

*Right:*
An unusual Edwardian postcard view inside the quarry. The locomotive is *Hugh Napier*, bought in 1904.
*Commercial postcard/Wrench/ Gwyn Price Collection*

*Below right:*
The oldest surviving Penrhyn de Winton, *George Henry*, built in Caernarfon in 1877 and seen in the quarry c1932. Last used in 1934, *George Henry* has been on display at the Narrow Gauge Railway Trust museum in Tywyn since 1956.
*H. M. Comber/ Festiniog Railway Archives*

Over the years over 30 steam locomotives were used in the port and quarries; this number included 13 of the distinctive 'quarry' Hunslet 0-4-0STs. Names applied were mostly those of Penrhyn family members. During the 1920s and 1930s 12 second-hand steam locomotives from different makers were also obtained. Some of these 'foreigners' had local antecedents, being obtained from Maenofferen, Cilgwyn and Dolgarrog, others had seen previous use as far away as Surrey and County Durham. The second-hand locomotives retained any existing names.

From 1932 the quarry workshops converted 18 motor cars for rail use; they appear to have fallen out of use, worn out, during the 1940s. Between 1946 and 1951 the quarry obtained or built 24 diesel locomotives. Two were home-made and the remainder were former Ministry of Supply Ruston & Hornsby locomotives. The quarry railways had all closed by early 1965. Many of the Penrhyn steam locomotives and a few of the diesels have been preserved. Despite the closure of the railway, the quarries continue in production under changed ownership.

*Left:*
*Pamela* in the 1930s; it was repainted and lined-out in 1938. *C. R. L. Coles*

*Below left:*
*Nesta* was new in 1899. Photographed on 25 June 1956, it was exported to the US in 1965. *Brian Hilton/ Millbrook House Collection*

*Above right:*
*Sybil Mary* in steam in the early 1950s. New in 1906, it was last used in 1955 and sold in 1966. *P. B. Whitehouse/ Millbrook House Collection*

*Centre right:*
*Edward Sholto* was new in 1909 and remained in service until 1956. The last new Penrhyn locomotive, *Edward Sholto* was exported to Canada in 1961. *P. B. Whitehouse/ Millbrook House Collection*

*Below right:*
*Hugh Napier* in action in the 1950s. Withdrawn for boiler repairs, never carried out, in 1954, *Hugh Napier* has been a member of the Penrhyn Castle collection since 1966. *Peter Johnson Collection*

*Left:*
*Lilla* was built in 1891 for the Cilgwyn Slate Quarry at Nantlle. Penrhyn purchased it for £150 in 1928. Its journey was made via the Bryngwyn incline and the Welsh Highland Railway to Dinas, on its own wheels, and then via LMS to Port Penrhyn. Photographed on 25 June 1956, it was not used after 1955 and was sold in 1963. *Lilla* is now owned by the Festiniog Railway Trust.
*Brian Hilton/ Millbrook House Collection*

*Centre left:*
*Marchlyn* was built by the Avonside Engine Co in Bristol in 1933 for the Durham County Water Board. It arrived at Penrhyn in 1936 and in 1965 was exported to the USA. The photograph was taken on 25 June 1956. *Brian Hilton/ Millbrook House Collection*

*Below left:*
*Eigiau* is an Orenstein & Koppel built in 1913. By 1917 it was working on the Cowlyd Reservoir Railway at Dolgarrog. It became surplus there in 1922 and was sold to Penrhyn in 1929. Almost immediately its cab and chimney were modified. It is seen at Port Penrhyn during the 1930s, posing with LMS '4F' No 4507 on one of the port's numerous mixed-gauge crossings. *H. W. Comber/ Festiniog Railway Archives*

*Above:*
*Winifred* at Port Penrhyn, c1951; apparently fresh out of works after an overhaul, this could be the occasion of its first steaming. The pipework is all new and the saddle tank is a new, welded and as yet unpainted replacement. One of the main line locos is in the shed. *P. B. Whitehouse/ Millbrook House Collection*

## Penmaenmawr

Unlike most other Welsh quarries, those at Penmaenmawr produced granite, not slate. Located on the North Wales coast between Llanfairfechan and Conwy, quarrying was first recorded on the side of Penmaenmawr Mountain, 1,545ft, from 1832. The Old and Graiglwyd Quarries were developed separately from the Penmaen East and West Quarries but all came into common ownership from 1911.

From the 1840s extensive networks of 3ft gauge railways were developed to connect the working areas to the LNWR's Chester & Holyhead Railway and to several piers along the coast, for a great deal of the quarries' output was consigned by sea; inclines connected different levels. The first locomotive was built on Anglesey, probably in the 1870s. Between 1878 and 1895 eight Caernarfon-built de Winton 0-4-0VBTs were used. In 1899 a Hunslet 0-4-0ST, a 3ft gauge version of the famous 'quarry' type, was obtained, although this one had inside instead of outside cylinders. Four more were bought before 1906. Adding variety, an Orenstein & Koppel 0-4-0WT was added to the fleet in 1907.

Following a trial with a home-made battery electric locomotive at some unknown date, some 13 internal combustion tractors were obtained between 1929 and 1941. The de Winton locomotives started to fall out of use during the 1930s and the Hunslets followed during the next decade. Three of the de Wintons survive, one on the mountain, one at Penrhyn Castle and one at Dinas station on the Welsh Highland Railway. All the Hunslet locomotives were scrapped; the tractors were either scrapped or sold for further use. The railways were taken out of use during the 1960s. The quarries are still in production.

*Left:*
1894-built de Winton *Harold* in steam in the early 1930s; it was dismantled by 1938.
*H. W. Comber/*
*Festiniog Railway Archives*

*Below left:*
3ft gauge 'quarry' Hunslet 0-4-0ST *Donald* in the early 1930s. Built in 1905, *Donald* was scrapped in 1951. Note the splendid acetylene lighting rig.
*H. W. Comber/*
*Festiniog Railway Archives*

## *Trefor*

The Trefor (Yr Eifl) Granite Quarry is one of Wales's lesser known industrial sites, located as it was on the north coast of the Lleyn Peninsula and all its output being exported by sea. Quarrying commenced under the auspices of Samuel Holland, better known for his links with Blaenau Ffestiniog and the development of the Festiniog Railway, in 1850. From 1911 the same company that owned the Penmaenmawr operation owned Trevor.

Two-foot gauge railways developed within the quarry and were linked by inclines, a further long and steep (1 in 1.75) one linking the quarry to Trevor village. Here a half-mile long railway to the pier came to be worked by locomotives. De Winton supplied the first two in 1873 and 1876. Two 0-4-0STs were then obtained: from

Bagnall in 1900 and from Hunslet in 1912. Second-hand machines were obtained in 1917 (a Kerr, Stewart 0-4-2ST), 1918 (a Hunslet 4-6-0T) and in 1921 an 0-4-0VBT. The latter was a home-made machine built by the Penmaenmawr foreman fitter for his boss's amusement around 1905. It did not stay long at Trevor but does have the distinction of being the only steam locomotive to work at Trevor that is still extant. The de Winton locomotives were scrapped by 1914, the others after 1930.

A fleet of petrol and diesel locomotives was obtained between 1918 and 1947. Some of these worked within the quarry but the railways there started to be replaced by roadways from 1951. Road vehicles replaced the main quarry incline and the main line to the pier in 1959 and conveyors replaced the pier railway in 1962. The quarry closed in 1971.

# Trefor (Yr Efail)

*Right:*
Trefor Granite Quarry's Hunslet 0-4-0ST *Betty* photographed in August 1933. Built in 1905, it was sold to Thomas Ward for further use in 1940, ending up at Brymbo Steel Co's Hook Norton ironstone quarry. (The chimney cap was cropped by the photographer.) *H. W. Comber/ Festiniog Railway Archives*

*Centre right:*
One of Trefor's Motor Rails shunting wagons to the pier railway in August 1933.
*H. W. Comber/ Festiniog Railway Archives*

*Below right:*
The remains of Bagnall 0-4-0ST *Isabel*. The locomotive was bought new in 1900 and was recorded scrapped in 1930.
*H. W. Comber/ Festiniog Railway Archives*

*Left:*
A typical Snowdon train waits to leave Llanberis in the early years. On the platform are supplies, bottled, for the Summit and at the window behind the wagon tea is on offer. *Francis Frith/ Millbrook House Collection*

*Centre left:*
No 3 *Wyddfa* at Llanberis on a fine afternoon with few passengers about.
*Commercial postcard/ Gwyn Price Collection*

*Below:*
This view from one of the railway's offices shows open fields, being harvested, behind the station. Passengers returning from their journey leave the station on foot while some have only a short journey to their motor car. In the platform is one of the 1924 coaches with one of the 1920s locomotives.
*Commercial postcard/Lilywhite/ Gwyn Price Collection*

# 12. Snowdon Mountain Railway

The Snowdon Mountain Railway is a Swiss mountain railway transposed to North Wales, unique here in both gauge and operation. The mountain is the highest peak in England and Wales, the railway on it being the first of those here described to be built exclusively for its current traffic — tourists.

The impetus for a railway to the summit of Snowdon followed the opening of the Carnarvon & Llanberis Railway in 1869, opening the village of Llanberis to tourists. In 1871 an announcement was made that a company had been formed to build a railway terminating at Crib-y-ddysgl, above Clogwyn and within 500ft of the summit. A different route was proposed in a Bill deposited in Parliament in 1874. Both schemes were dependent on access to land owned by George William Duff Assheton-Smith, who owned all

of the north face of the mountain, and much else, including the Dinorwic Quarries, besides. Assheton-Smith objected to the railway schemes, fearing for the interests of his tenants, some of whom supplemented their incomes by

*Below:*
Passengers sometimes arrived at the railway by charabanc, as seen on 30 May 1922. Creams of Llandudno was running tours to Welsh narrow gauge railways until at least the late 1970s; its uniformed driver has his back to the camera to the left of the ground frame. The signal and ground frame were supplied for the opening by the Railway Signal Co. The post was removed in the 1930s but the ground frame is still in position, hidden by the line's control office. One of the original carriages, with its roof boards removed, is in the platform. *Gwyn Price Collection*

providing services to those who did visit the mountain and who could afford to pay for them.

The opening of the North Wales Narrow Gauge Railways to Rhyd Ddu brought about another proposal and was ultimately responsible for a change in attitudes. That line's temporary terminus at Quellyn Lake was named Snowdon from opening in 1878 and Snowdon Ranger in 1881. The permanent terminus at Rhyd Ddu was renamed Snowdon in 1893, all these names of course emphasising proximity to Snowdon. Rhyd Ddu is 626ft above sea level, compared to Llanberis's 353ft, theoretically requiring less climbing. However, despite Rhyd Ddu being 5 miles from the summit and Llanberis being only 3¼ miles, eliminating the height benefit, the NWNGR was able to siphon off some of the Llanberis tourist trade. In 1881, in anticipation of this traffic from the NWNGR, Charles Easton Spooner and John Sylvester Hughes, both then working for the Festiniog Railway, announced a proposal for a Rhyd Ddu—Snowdon Summit—Llanberis rack railway. Nothing came of this scheme either.

Assheton-Smith's attitude had clearly changed by 1894 when the Snowdon Mountain Tramroad & Hotels Co Ltd was registered as a public company, obviously with his tacit support because his agent was one of the company's promoters! The company was empowered to build a railway up the mountain from Llanberis, with a hotel at the summit, and to take over the Royal Victoria Hotel, owned by Assheton-Smith, at Llanberis. The railway was to be a rack line built to the 'Abt' principle. The issue of 6,343 £10 shares and 200 £100 4½ % debentures financed the railway.

Construction started in December 1894, the first sod being cut by Assheton-Smith's daughter. Legal powers were not required because all the land required was owned by Assheton-Smith.

The first Manager and Secretary of SMT&H was Gowrie Aitchison. Of the railways covered in this book, Aitchison was involved at different times with the NWNGR, the Portmadoc, Beddgelert & South Snowdon Railway, the Welsh Highland Railway and the Great Orme Tramway. He was also to be an officer of the North Wales Power & Traction Co! He stayed with the SMR until 1910, even then being retained as consultant engineer.

Three steam locomotives were ordered from Schweizerische Lokomotiv und Maschinenfabrik (SLM) of Winterthür, Switzerland, and were delivered in 1895. They were nominally 0-4-2Ts, except that all traction forces were transmitted through axle-mounted pinions to the rack, the wheels being actually loose on their axles. The boilers are inclined in the frames, the inclination preventing the firebox being damaged when the locomotive

*Left:*
No 8 *Eryri* shunts an empty
coach, rebodied and almost
fully glazed since the war, into
the departure platform on 18
June 1955. The coach in the
arrival platform has merely
been improved by glazing the
end. *F. W. Shuttleworth*

*Above right:*
No 4 *Snowdon* shunts the
undercarriage of one of the 19th
century locomotives, 1932.
*W. H. Whitworth/
Gwyn Price Collection*

*Centre right:*
No 4 again, with draught
excluders fitted, and one of the
original carriages. The wagons
contain bricks; they might have
been for the new summit
building, completed in 1936.
The railway had four of these
wagons in 1896 but they saw
very little use; only one
survives.
*Millbrook House Collection*

*Below right:*
Refuelling. No 5 *Moel Siabod*
has been equipped with a more
substantial draught excluder,
complete with a sliding hatch
for the handbrake handle.
*Millbrook House Collection*

was on the gradient, a standard practice on mountain railways. They were numbered and named, No 1 *L. A. D. A. S.* (Laura Alice Duff Assheton-Smith, Assheton-Smith's daughter), No 2 *Enid* and No 3 *Wyddfa*. The contractor used the first locomotives to transport materials during construction.

Four carriages were ordered from the Lancaster Railway Carriage & Wagon Co; they were semi-opens built to Swiss specifications. In 1896 two more locomotives were received, No 4 *Snowdon* and No 5 *Moel Siabod*. Two more coaches were obtained at the same time. One of the bogies on each coach was fitted with a brake pinion that engaged if the speed exceeded a pre-set limit. Its efficiency was amply demonstrated on 6 April 1896 as will be seen. There was no coupling between carriage and locomotive.

The use of steam was considered to be provisional as electricity was actively considered during construction; indeed a local newspaper headed its report on the 'first sod' ceremony, 'The Snowdon Electric Railway'. The finished railway was 800mm (2ft 7½ in) gauge and 4½ miles long with a ruling gradient of 1 in 5½ .

The official opening took place on Easter Monday 1896. Despite the successful operation of numerous works and test trains, disaster struck. The locomotive of the first public down train left the rails just above Clogwyn and fell down the mountainside, damaging the telegraph as it did so. The breaking telegraph cables short-circuited, causing the telegraph bell at the summit to ring. The crew of the train waiting there took this as the signal to leave. They did so in fog and ran into the carriages of the first train. A man who had jumped off the first train and fallen under it, later died of his injuries. The passengers of both trains had to walk back to Llanberis. While investigations into the cause of the accident got under way the company suspended all operations.

It was eventually decided that some slight settlement of the track was probably the cause of the locomotive climbing the rack. To prevent a repetition, flanged guard-rails were fitted to the rack, the modification being completed before the railway was reopened to the public. After the 1896 accident a second, independent, brake was also fitted to the carriages. On 19 April 1897, just over a year after the accident, the railway reopened. Considerable effort was put in to publicise the railway; the response showed that the accident was no deterrent. The additional safety precautions taken were probably a great morale booster.

locomotive *Padarn* in 1924. Two orders for two
new carriages each were placed with the Swiss
company Schweizerische Industrie-Gesellschaft
(SIG); it is unclear if both orders were fulfilled.
Delivery of at least two vehicles took place in
1924.

The company was restructured in 1928 and
was renamed the Snowdon Mountain Railway
Ltd. Since 1923 the Board of Directors has
always included at least one member of the
Davies family, Pwllheli-based solicitors who
also had interests in the Festiniog and Welsh
Highland Railways at that time.

Unlike many other organisations, the SMR
made profits during the 1930s and entered
World War 2 in good order, although it could
not afford to have No 4 *Snowdon* overhauled in
1939; there was no immediate need for it then
anyway. During World War 2 the summit
buildings were taken over by different sections
of the armed forces and many trains were
operated On His Majesty's Service. The
operation, or not, of a passenger service
appeared to depend upon the whims of the
current tenants of the summit but no trains
were run for the public from the end of 1943.

After the cessation of hostilities public
services were not resumed until 1946 due to a
shortage of supplies and labour. Lack of
attention during the war meant that
considerable effort was required to overcome
the arrears of maintenance. The coaches were
rebuilt with new, fully enclosed bodies, one
being dealt with at Llanberis each year from
1951. From 1956 a programme of locomotive
overhauls was commenced, the four oldest
being sent, one each year from 1958, to Hunslet
in Leeds for the work to be carried out; work on
the others, including firebox replacement, was
undertaken at Llanberis and this is the current
practice. The track was relaid throughout from
1967. Mortgages were taken out to finance some
of this work but ultimately it was only possible
because the public still wanted to travel to the
summit of Snowdon by train.

Originally the locomotives propelled two
carriages up the line but some time after the
reopening a single carriage became the norm.
By 1900 two open carriages were in use, either
together or in combination with the semi-open
cars.

The debentures issued to finance construction
became due for repayment in 1915, in the midst
of World War 1. Although the railway continued
operating, the receipts were on the low side, so
an agreement was obtained which delayed
repayment for five years, with extra interest
being paid. By the 1920s the railway was
sufficiently well off to buy additional rolling
stock; SLM was again the source of three new
locomotives, up-to-date versions of the first
ones. Delivered in 1922/3, they were No 6 *Sir
Harmood*, No 7 *Aylwin* and No 8 *Eryri*. No 6 was
named after the company's former chairman,
Sir Harmood Banner; a new board renamed the

*Left:*
Clogwyn, with No 5 *Moel Siabod* waiting to pass No 4 *Snowdon*. In this early photograph a crest has been affixed to the carriage side. *Commercial postcard/ Gwyn Price Collection*

*Above:*
No 5 and train at Clogwyn between the wars, on what was obviously a warm day with only a light breeze; the area behind and below the train was known as the 'valley of hats'! The layout of the original coaches is well presented in this photograph; they seated eight passengers in each compartment. *H. Gordon Tidey/ Loco Publishing Co*

*Left:*
No 7 *Aylwin* waits at Clogwyn in the 1950s. *Commercial postcard/J. Valentine/ Peter Johnson Collection*

*Right:*
Approaching the Summit. The lake, Llyn Ffynnon-y-gwas, is a reservoir.
*Commercial postcard/H. Barton/ Peter Johnson Collection*

*Centre right:*
Summit platform on a busy day between the wars; the actual summit is 60ft higher.
*Commercial postcard/J. Salmon/ Peter Johnson Collection*

*Below right:*
No 3 *Wyddfa* at the Summit on 18 June 1955. The carriage has been rebuilt but is still not fully glazed. The station building was designed by Clough Williams-Ellis and opened in 1936. *F. W. Shuttleworth*

Above:
No 5, lettered 'Great Orme Tramways', on Ty Gwyn Road when the tramway was very new, showing the track arrangement on a section where the cars could never cross each other. The overhead wires were for communication purposes. *Commercial postcard/ Photochrom/Peter Johnson Collection*

Below:
No 4 just above the passing loop in Ty Gwyn Road; No 5 is visible at Black Gate. In this picture No 4 is lettered 'Great Orme Railway'. *Commercial postcard/ J. Valentine/Peter Johnson Collection*

# 13. Great Orme Tramway

The Great Orme Tramway owes its distinction to being the only British cable funicular tramway.

Opened in 1902 (the lower section) and 1903 (the upper section), the 3ft 6in gauge tramway operates up the 679ft-high Great Orme headland at Llandudno. Built under powers granted by the Great Orme Tramways Act of 1898, the tramway is a rope-hauled system, with two Hurst Nelson-built cars on each half-mile section. The winding house is at the Half Way station. When built the tramway was equipped with two steam-powered winding engines, one for each section; the steam plant was replaced by an electric system after the 1957 season. Passengers undertaking the whole journey alight at the Half Way station to transfer from one section to the other. The lower section is a street tramway while the upper runs across open country. A passing place on each section allows a 6min service to operate at peak times.

A runaway on the lower section in 1932 had serious implications for the operators. It was found to have been caused by a broken drawbar and aggravated by disconnected emergency brakes. The accident left two dead and 10 seriously injured. On discovering the details of the deactivated brakes, actually made inoperative in 1906, the insurance company renounced the company's policy, forcing it into liquidation to avoid £14,000 in claims made by passengers. By agreement with the Tramway Company's creditors the liquidator was able to get a new emergency brake system installed and resumed operating in 1934. At the end of that year the tramway was sold to the Great Orme Railway Company; from 1935 the cars were lettered 'Great Orme Railway' accordingly. In 1949 Llandudno Urban District Council exercised the powers granted it in the 1898 Act and bought the tramway. It has remained in local authority ownership ever since.

*Right:*
No 5 seen within the restricted confines of Old Road.
*Commercial postcard/Lilywhite/
Peter Johnson Collection*

*Left:*
One of the 1907-built cars climbing Penrhyn Hill over the Little Orme before 1910; the line's steepest gradients were on this section.
*Commercial Postcard/*
*Pictorial Stationery Co/*
*Peter Johnson Collection*

*Centre left:*
Llandudno-bound No 14, the last of the 1907 trams, leaves one of the passing loops on the original single line between the two towns; the track was doubled by 1930.
*Commercial postcard/*
*Peter Johnson Collection*

*Below left:*
The photographer rides on the top deck of a double-deck car to photograph No 2 at Bodafon Fields on 12 August 1939.
*S. Newton/*
*Peter Johnson Collection*

*Right:*
No 7, a former Bournemouth car, in Abergele Road, Colwyn Bay on 28 May 1946. The lower deck appears to be well-laden but there are few prospective passengers in the street; notice the portent of things to come, the line of parked cars behind.
*E. C. Haywood/*
*Peter Johnson Collection*

# 14. Llandudno & Colwyn Bay Electric Railway

Until 1956 Llandudno was blessed with two narrow gauge tramways. The Llandudno & Colwyn Bay Electric Railway was, at its maximum, an 8½ -mile line linking the two popular North Wales seaside resorts, its early history as complex as some of the other lines described in the book.

The first section of the Llandudno & Colwyn Bay route, between Llandudno West Shore Parade and the depot at Rhos-on-Sea, five miles, was opened in 1907. A further 1½ -mile section from Rhos to Station Road, Colwyn Bay, was opened the following year. This statement of openings is deceptive, for it conceals the length of time it took for a company to have sufficient resources to get the tramway built.

Proposals for a tramway to link the towns were first made in 1894. A Light Railway Order was made in 1899. In addition to the Llandudno — Colwyn Bay route the Order empowered a route onwards to Rhyl and Prestatyn that was never built. A deviation Order was obtained in 1903 and a contract was placed for the Llandudno — Rhos Depot section in 1904. No work was carried out however. A new company formed in 1906 failed the same year, after having started work. Another company formed in 1906, the Llandudno & District Electric Tramway Construction Co, took over the assets and obligations and succeeded in getting the line opened late in 1907. The Construction Company's contractor was Bruce Peebles & Co,

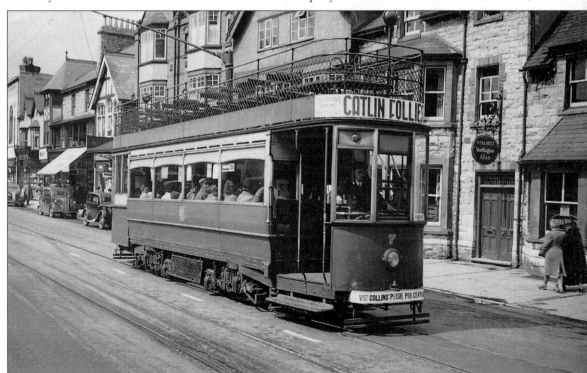

at that time engaged on the Portmadoc, Beddgelert & South Snowdon Railway around Beddgelert.

The line between Rhos Depot and Colwyn Bay was authorised by a Light Railway Order made in 1907. At either extremity the tramway was street-running, while between the towns there were sections of reserved unpaved track and a section along a private toll road. The most notable feature of the route was the 1 in 11½ gradient at Penrhynside. Built as a single line with passing loops, most of the route was converted to double track between 1912 and 1928. Fourteen single-deck tramcars were obtained from the Midland Railway Carriage & Wagon Co of Shrewsbury to operate the service.

Two further Light Railway Orders, made in 1907 and 1912, authorised, *inter alia*, a further extension, 1¼ miles to Old Colwyn, opened in 1915. This section was never a commercial success and most of it was abandoned in 1929, a victim of competing buses. The short section on West Shore Promenade was abandoned in 1917.

The Construction Co became the Llandudno & Colwyn Bay Electric Railway Co in 1909. The fleet was augmented by four semi-convertible cars obtained from the United Electric Car Co of Preston the same year. In recognition of the tramway's seaside location, an order for four open toastrack cars was placed in 1914, although World War 1 delayed delivery from

English Electric until 1920. These vehicles were the last built new for the company, future acquisitions being second-hand. Five single-deck trams were obtained from Accrington Corporation in 1931 and 10 double-deck open-top trams from Bournemouth Corporation in 1936.

A reduction in road competition caused by fuel rationing contributed to an increase in tramway traffic during World War 2. In 1946 two streamlined double-deck cars were obtained from Darwen Corporation. These modern-looking vehicles were restricted from operating over Penrhyn Hill due to Ministry of Transport fears that they were at risk of being blown over and their brakes were inadequate.

In the 1950s passenger numbers went into decline and the tramway operated at a loss. In 1955 the company decided to terminate the tram service and operate the route with motor buses instead, the last day eventually occurring on 24 March 1956. The tramway was the last privately owned narrow gauge public street tramway in Britain.

*Below:*
Car No 17, originally No 14, at the Mostyn Street/Gloddaeth Street ('Palladium Corner') stop in Llandudno on 19 June 1945. *E. C. Haywood/Peter Johnson Collection*

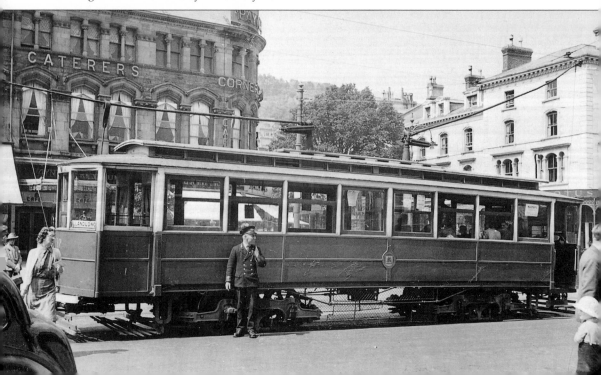

# 15. Rhyl Marine Lake Miniature Railway

The shortest railway in this book, the Rhyl Marine Lake Miniature Railway played a significant role in the development of public miniature railways, being designed by Henry Greenly, who later went on to design the Romney, Hythe & Dymchurch Railway for Captain Howey.

The Rhyl line's sponsor was Miniature Railways (Great Britain) Ltd, a company promoted by W. J. Bassett-Lowke, the Northampton-based model railway builder. Established in 1904, the company had built, equipped and operated several 15in gauge railways, including several temporary exhibition lines.

Opened to the public on 1 May 1911, the 15in gauge track ran around a marine-water lake; Henry Greenly surveyed the line and designed the layout and buildings. A Greenly-designed Bassett-Lowke locomotive, 4-4-2 *Prince Edward of Wales*, was allocated to the line. Previously named *Red Dragon*, it had been built in 1909

when it had worked at the White City Exhibition. The change of name was to take advantage of publicity accruing from the institution of HRH Prince Edward as Prince of Wales at Caernarfon shortly after the railway opened.

Before the end of the first season Miniature Railways (Great Britain) Ltd was placed into voluntary liquidation and the railway was taken over by Narrow Gauge Railways Ltd, another Bassett-Lowke company. In 1912 ownership of the railway passed to Rhyl Amusements Ltd, the owner of the adjoining amusement park. A second Bassett-Lowke 4-4-2, *George the Fifth*, and a second set of coaches, built by the new owner,

*Below:*
A train of three of the six bogie coaches made in Rhyl after the railway was taken over by Rhyl Amusements Ltd in 1912; these coaches allowed all passengers to sit facing the same direction.
*Commercial postcard/Peter Johnson Collection*

*Left:*
Early days, c1912, on the Rhyl Marine Lake Miniature Railway, the first of its type in Wales. The driver has a young girl with him on the footplate of Bassett-Lowke 4-4-2 *Prince Edward of Wales* and everyone looks at the photographer, so some things don't change.
*Commercial postcard/J. Valentine/ Peter Johnson Collection*

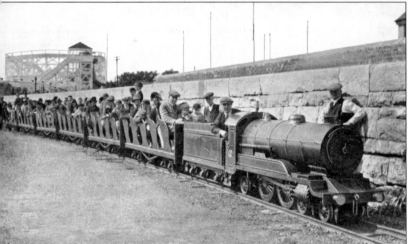

*Centre left:*
By the time of this view, July 1930, passengers' fashions had changed considerably but everyone still wore a hat.
*Commercial postcard/J. Valentine/ Peter Johnson Collection*

*Below left:*
Another view of a typical Barnes train, produced to promote both the railway and its operator. The styles of dress show that the photograph was not taken on the sort of day you would seek to promote a seaside resort and its attractions.
*Commercial postcard/ Peter Johnson Collection*

were provided. *George the Fifth* was built in 1911 and operated at Southport before being transferred to Rhyl. Rhyl Amusements commissioned Greenly to design a new, more powerful, locomotive that could be built locally. A. Barnes & Co, the family company of Albert Barnes, Rhyl Amusements' manager, built six of these between 1920 and 1934, two being sold to other operators. *Prince Edward of Wales* left Rhyl in 1920 and *George the Fifth* in 1922.

The railway was closed and lifted in 1969 and then reinstated on a slightly different alignment in 1978. Only one of the Barnes-built locomotives is on site; others are still to be found in Wales.

# 16. Glyn Valley Tramway

This is probably the strangest of the lines featured in this book, by virtue of its gauge, roadside location and its motive power. Although located to the east of the other railways herein described, it came about, like most of them, by the need to get minerals to market more efficiently.

Attempts were first made to connect the slate quarrying centre of Glyn Ceiriog to the market town of Chirk, both in Denbighshire, from the mid-19th century. An attempt to build a combined turnpike road and tramway failed but with the Cambrian Slate Co paying half the cost the turnpike was built, opening in 1863; the road was made wide enough to accommodate a tramway at a later date. An Act obtained in 1866 authorised a standard gauge railway from Glyn Ceiriog to Ellesmere; the collapses of Thomas Savin, promoting what became the Cambrian Railways, and of the Gurney

Overend Bank that same year, were responsible for no action being taken in the Glyn Valley. An Amendment Act obtained in 1869 truncated the Ellesmere line back to a terminus with the GWR at Preesgwyn, south of Chirk, and converted it to narrow gauge, reducing the estimated cost from £125,000 to £25,000, but still no action was taken. In 1870 the tramway idea was revived, influenced by the 1870 Tramways Act, and the Glyn Valley Tramway Act was obtained the same year.

*Below:*
Beyer Peacock 0-4-2 *Glyn*, ordered in 1891, at Chirk station. The Great Western Railway station is over the wall to the left. The fine array of vehicles in the GVT train includes two opens and a van.
*Loco Publishing Co*

The tramway had the unique gauge of
2ft 4¼in, exactly half that of the standard gauge,
and almost certainly chosen because Glyn
Ceiriog Quarries used that gauge on their
internal tramways. It opened in 1873 for freight,
mainly slate and granite, and 1874 for
passengers. The original eastern terminus was
at Pontfaen, southwest of Chirk, from where a
tramway connected with the GWR between
Chirk and Preesgwyn, and the Shropshire
Union Canal, a total distance of eight miles.

Despite being a roadside tramway it was at
first a gravity line, horses pulling the empties
back to the quarries. An Act of 1885, among
other things, authorised a diversion from
Pontfaen to Chirk, where convenient
interchange was formed alongside the GWR's
station there and a new interchange was created
with the Shropshire Union Canal.

The 1885 Act also authorised the use of steam
traction, to accommodate which the tramway
was relaid, becoming 2ft 4½ in gauge in the
process. In 1888 the first of three Beyer Peacock
0-4-2 tram engines arrived, the second
following in 1889 and the third in 1892. To
complete the GVT's locomotive story, an ex-
military Baldwin 4-6-0T was obtained in 1921.
The Chirk deviation was opened to passengers,
with steam traction, in 1891; the 45-minute
single journey time for horse power was
reduced to 35 minutes with steam.

In this guise the Glyn Valley Tramway served
its community quite well. It endeavoured to
promote itself and its environs, as this text of a
1911 advertisement *(right)* demonstrates:

*Above:*
*Sir Theodore* at Pontfadog in the mid-1920s. The locomotive was built in 1888 and did not have a complete front cabsheet.
*A. W. Croughton/*
*Millbrook House Collection*

*Right:*
Facing a motive power crisis after World War 1, the GVT bought a war surplus Baldwin 4-6-0PT in 1921 and sent it to Beyer Peacock to be adapted to GVT purposes, including regauging from 60cm. It was photographed at Glyn Ceiriog on 31 May 1932, four years before it was scrapped.
*H. C. Casserley/*
*Millbrook House Collection*

# Finale

*Above:*

It has already been remarked that many of the railways featured in this book owed their origins and existence to mineral traffic. These two final photographs are included as reminders of this fact, and of the Festiniog Railway's staple, and profit-making, traffic for so many years.

The Oakeley Quarry was a major player in the Blaenau Ffestiniog slate trade and the part of it owned by Samuel Holland was the first to send its output via the FR. This postcard shows two of the quarry's inclines, the one on the left connecting with the FR's Dinas branch. The famous bridge was used to transport slate waste to the Glan-y-don tip, now removed. The LNWR had part of it reinforced when its Conwy Valley line reached the town in 1881, deeming the original timber piers a hazard to its operations. *Commercial postcard/ Glyn Price Collection*

*Left:*

The identity of this Blaenau Ffestiniog quarry has yet to be established. Captioned to show quarrymen leaving work, it also shows an incline gripper wagon and several rubbish wagons.*Commercial postcard/ Glyn Price Collection*